TRIALS to TRIUMPH

A True Story of Faith and Hope

Kristine Diana Schroeder 4/16/17

Tonja,
Let his light shine...
even in the
trials!
Kristine Schroeder

WESTBOW
P R E S S®
A DIVISION OF THOMAS NELSON
& ZONDERVAN

Scripture quotations from the New Revised Standard Version Bible, copyright © 1989,
Division of Christian Education of the National Council of the Churches of
Christ in the United States of America. Used by permission. All rights reserved.

Scripture quotations from the Holy Bible, NEW INTERNATIONAL VERSION®.
Copyright © 1973, 1978, 1984, 2011 by Biblica, Inc. All rights reserved worldwide.
Used by permission. NEW INTERNATIONAL VERSION® and NIV® are
registered trademarks of Biblica, Inc. Use of either trademark for the offering
of goods or services requires the prior written consent of Biblica US, Inc.

Scripture quotations from The Message.
Copyright © by Eugene H. Peterson 1993, 1994, 1995, 1996, 2000,
2001, 2002. Used by permission of NavPress Publishing Group.

WestBow Press books may be ordered through booksellers or by contacting:

WestBow Press
A Division of Thomas Nelson & Zondervan
1663 Liberty Drive
Bloomington, IN 47403
www.westbowpress.com
1 (866) 928-1240

ISBN: 978-1-5127-1885-0 (sc)
ISBN: 978-1-5127-1886-7 (hc)
ISBN: 978-1-5127-1884-3 (e)

Library of Congress Control Number: 2015918319

Print information available on the last page.

WestBow Press rev. date: 12/17/2015

Dedication

This book is dedicated to all who endure trials in life, yet continue to search for purpose and understanding. May you one day learn that God has already prepared a way for you to know and understand your purpose. It is God who always triumphs over our trials!

Contents

Acknowledgements

As life is, this book has been a process. So, even though it is completed, it commences another stage of the journey. The pages of this book reflect the pages of my heart, soul, spirit, body, and mind as lived out in my life.

This dream has been encouraged by many. "Thank you" does not seem enough to commemorate the love, encouragement, and support I have been given to proceed with my writing.

Deepest gratitude is given to: my husband, Bill, for recognizing my gifts long before I could and loving me through all the hills and valleys we have endured together; my editor and dearest friend, Laura, who through so many trials has helped me keep my sanity and perspective; my parents for sharing their faith and encouragement through all life sent my way; the Rev. Larry H.T. Johnson for his quiet inspiration and continual trust in God's power, and to my Lord who has proven time and time again that His triumph truly does conquer every trial!

Prologue

When it comes to what I believe, I base my thoughts and words on the lifelong faith that continues to develop in me. Through life experiences, my theology has grown and expanded. But I note that over time there have been many questions, doubts, and misunderstandings, as well as answers, reassurances, and hard-earned wisdom. Faith has urged me to question that which I believe, which is the key to the whole concept of faith. I believe that God wants us to be certain of what we believe, so that we can better and more effectively proclaim the Gospel. We can only learn and grow when we question and seek understanding about that which we face with clouded vision and muffled hearing.

When I question the things that I believe in order to better understand a difficult situation, I must consider that which I am surrounded by in my life so to better comprehend my faith in God. My Christian faith is certainly not limited to the words of Scripture. God created this great big world and all that it contains, so we might be blessed with even a glimpse of His power, wonder, and grace.

To be honest, I fail daily to understand and appreciate the glory and splendor of God. I fail daily in my life, for that matter. But I am assured by my faith as it grows from glory to glory.

Personally, I have dealt with a lot of trials in my life. It is God's grace and my faith which have pulled me through these situations.

I have discovered that I need hard times. I do not learn or grow without them. I thank God for these times, but not often enough.

This story begins in the summer of 1969. It is a story borne out of the words in Romans and the grace of God.

> *Therefore, since we are justified by faith, we have peace with God through our Lord Jesus Christ, through whom we have obtained access to this grace in which we stand; and we boast in our hope of sharing the glory of God. And not only that, but we also boast in our sufferings, knowing that suffering produces endurance, and endurance produces character, and character produces hope, and hope does not disappoint us, because God's love has been poured into our hearts through the Holy Spirit that has been given to us. (Romans 5:1-5, NRSV)*

My parents and older brother, Mike, lived in Lancaster, California. They were active at Lutheran Church of the Master, and my mom was expecting her second baby. We've often joked that it all began with a sneeze, when my mom's water broke. You see, they lived in the high desert and the wind was always blowing. My mom is allergic to what often seems like everything. So when the wind blew, her allergies flourished.

The stories I have been told never spoke of a miserable pregnancy, labor, or delivery. Considering all that women know today about their unborn child, it is sometimes difficult to understand the day I was born. Even after I was delivered, my mother did not know anything was wrong. I can only imagine what the doctors and nurses thought when they first saw me: fear, shock, disgust, and concern for my survival- this I will never know. What they saw was a baby, just under six pounds, with uneven limbs, many profound birthmarks, and tumors bulging from within her body. Someone, perhaps a doctor, looked at my mother and asked her accusatorily "What medication did you take while you were pregnant?" How afraid and responsible she must have felt even though she had only done as her doctor had instructed.

The pages of this book tell the story of trials that followed that shocking question one hot summer day and how trials were overcome by God's strength, love, and grace - a story which continues to blossom and grow each day. My hope is that you will be inspired to actively seek God's triumph through all the trials that come your way.

A Foundation of
Faith and Hope

Many people can pinpoint the exact time in their life when their faith literally came to life! Perhaps it was a time when God became so present that there was absolutely no question whether God was real. Others may describe their faith as something that gently appeared over time. Whether God enters a life roaring like a lion or gamboling like a lamb, God enters at the divine time selected by what is best for the individual. I have heard people say, "God must have left me because terrible things continue to happen." I truly believe that God is not watching from a far off corner as bad things happen in our lives or the world. God is not about playing games with our emotions and lives. Instead, I believe God is walking the journey of this life with us, and weeps when we face pain or difficulty.

Interestingly, I do not find the development of my personal faith like either of the two scenarios described above. I have not been able to find an exact moment in time when my faith came to life. Alternately, I do have some context that would support God gently appearing over time. However, I believe my faith journey is a slight combination of the two - instantly coming to life and gently nourished over time.

O Lord, you have searched me and known me.
You know when I sit down and when I rise up;

you discern my thoughts from far away.
You search out my path and my lying down,
and are acquainted with all my ways.
For it was you who formed my inward parts;
you knit me together in my mother's womb.
I praise you, for I am fearfully and wonderfully made.
(Psalm 139:1-3; 13-14a, NRSV)

Psalm 139 has been read to me and by me on numerous occasions throughout my life. Each time I am reminded of the intricate nature in which God created every part of me, long before I was born. Another portion of this Psalm not referenced above completes the focus God has on our lives. Many times it is called the Psalm of the Inescapable God. Even when we feel as if God is playing hide and seek with us, He is not far off in unknown lands. God is nearer still to every step we take.

The foundation of my faith and hope has been formed throughout my life through each and every experience. I was encouraged at a young age to ask questions, and verbalize my doubts and misunderstandings, with the reassurance that all these would help form my beliefs. Within the development of my faith, I was strongly encouraged by my parents, Sunday School teachers, and pastor to dare to ask questions and seek the answers God provided. I believe God wants us to be certain of what we believe, in order that we might better and more effectively proclaim the Good News to the places our lives take us. In my eyes, we can only learn and grow to understand when we take the time and energy to question and seek the understanding of that which we face with cluttered eyes and ears.

I often remind myself that in order to better comprehend my faith in God I must take into account that which surrounds me in my life. Many factors have aided me in creating the foundation of my faith and hope. My Christian faith and understanding are not limited to the thin pages of my Bible. I believe that God created this world and all that is in it so that we might be able to grasp even a glimpse of the wonder of God.

As I was nurtured in my younger years to deepen and broaden my faith, I tended to focus on what I could do to help others. My denomination invites young people to become adult members of the church sometime before they graduate from high school. When I was in the ninth grade, I had this opportunity after additional education and service. My class decided on the theme "Confirmed in Hope." We were affirming the faith our parents/ guardians had baptized us into some years before, with hope for our future.

One of the ways we prepared before the actual ceremony of affirming our faith was to formulate our thoughts about faith and hope into an essay. This expressed what our faith meant to us, how it developed, and what we hoped it would look like in the future. I wrote that I wanted a chance in my life to deepen my knowledge of Christ and become a more understanding person. It was also my hope that the world would be a better place and that the people of this world would learn to trust God to bring them through troublesome times.

When considering the future of our faith and hope we were to ponder what we wanted to do and how we saw it taking shape. I had great hopes at the age of fourteen. I wanted to help our church by taking on just about every task within and outside its walls. By serving in worship, education, and the everyday life of the church, I hoped to make a difference. Ultimately I wanted to serve and help others know God. Our pastor read some of our hopes in worship the day of our confirmation. He noted that I was taking on a lot for such a young person. I felt as if my hopes and dreams for my faith in action were very achievable - after all, I had been very involved in the church since the day I was born.

I called my mom one day from college and spoke to her about a concern of mine. I realized one afternoon that I had already achieved my hopes and dreams for my faith that had been set into motion less than ten years prior when I affirmed my faith. My faith had truly been put into action, and now I needed to look forward to new hopes and dreams. At this time I re-examined my faith, God's presence, and what God was truly guiding me to do. I understood that my faith and hope would continue to be molded and strengthened for the future by God's eternal grace and love. What I had learned would help me teach and reach out to others and lead them by the same example of grace and love.

During my ministry when I taught teenagers, I always encouraged them to attempt to teach those younger than themselves. If a person can teach what they have learned to someone who has less knowledge of the topic, the teacher can gain insight into how well they themselves have learned the material. If one is able to teach well, one learns better ways of describing the thought or story by utilizing a language easily understood by the learner. In addition, the easier one can answer questions about the topic, the better the teacher knows the subject at hand. This allows the topic to be engrained in the mind of any individual.

One of the most profound facets of my faith that I have learned is that my faith is strengthened during difficult times. Sure, I have times of being angry, frustrated, fearful, and lonely, but without these times, it can be difficult to be thankful for the times of wonder and beauty. It has been said that if a person does not know joy, safety, or love it is difficult for him or her to understand another's sadness, fear, or hate. The lows of life aid us in comprehending the full spectrum of life and its experiences.

The life of Jesus provided this example for me. Jesus too had very difficult and trying times in His life on earth. These provided opportunities for Him to share the power of God through His actions. Jesus, also called Rabbi or Teacher, utilized parables to get His point across. Parables are often noted as being a story to help make a point. Some see parables as childish or insignificant due to their simplicity. On the contrary, I see them as very real and significant. Jesus has a message to get across to those who dare to listen. He utilizes stories people can relate to in their own lives. If a story causes one to ponder, consider, or make a change for the better, then it is certainly not "simple." This was the purpose of Jesus's ministry: to bring about a change in the hearts of the people. And yes, hearts changed.

The hearts of the people can and will continue to change as long as the status quo is challenged. Jesus's earthly ministry provided a great example of life-freeing faith and hope. Jesus's communication style utilized a variety of approaches depending on what needed to be said and who needed to hear it. Jesus's varying degrees of communication were not limited to questioning, listening, telling, and keeping silence. In addition, Jesus used His own personal examples to provide direction to those who listened because the hearer is often touched on a deeper level when personal examples are used. Jesus utilized important care when teaching the Good News. Jesus was not afraid to question those around Him in order to pique their interest and then simply guide them along the right path.

Jesus is the prime example for us to receive direction in our lives, troubled or not. So often we are struck down by the burdens of our lives that we forget Jesus too lived a miserable life and died a more miserable death. Jesus is our perfect, personal, real-life example of a human who endured pain and suffering amidst a changing world and was still able to focus on what God wanted Him to do. Jesus had patience, understanding, and the knack for getting to the point in a gentle yet straight forward approach. Jesus is our example. We can model our lives after His. We can be guaranteed that we will never be as proper, concrete, or precise as Jesus, but He provides for us a place to begin our growth process. By searching the depths of Jesus's heart and intent, we can find the building blocks to build our own foundation of faith and hope. Personally, it has always comforted me to know that Jesus endured similar physical and emotional pain in His life. More importantly, I am reminded that He walks beside me during my life in order to endure it with me all over again. By this act, Jesus brings a comfort to me that reminds me of how much I am loved by God. I am never alone. When things look gloomy and I feel alone, I am invited to seek the heart of this compassionate teacher to model for each of us what life is all about: loving, hoping, and developing faith through the pain.

Recently I came in contact with a novice painter. I was deeply struck by the emotion that was portrayed in each painting. The strokes of paint enticed my heart to seek God's magnitude and solace in nature and the depths of God's heart. Two paintings in particular caught my eye and spoke deeply to my soul. Both were pictures of Jesus: Jesus at peace lying in the tomb, and the suffering Jesus hanging on the cross. Both pictures were only of His face. The shadowing of the first reminded me of the calm and peace after the storm. When we have endured difficult situations, our spirit needs rest and a time to connect with the heart of God. The second painting spoke to the storms of my life. It is a visible reminder of the pain Jesus endured and a true representation that all of my pain was taken to the cross, so that I might believe and have eternal life knowing I am never alone.

God not only came to each of us through Jesus Christ, but God continues to come to us through each other. I am an optimistic person who tends to believe in the goodness of each person. I also believe through Jesus we each can help make a difference in this world. My faith is a very complex part of who I am and my very existence. I also have a greater understanding of who God is with each new day. God is a vast part of this world we live in, the One who continues to create new and wonderful things every day. I am certain that I will always have questions for God about where I am to go and what is right. By looking at the living example of Jesus, I see the life of the world's greatest teacher. When it comes to having faith and hope, I know that I do not have all of the answers. More importantly, I do not need all the answers. With each new day my understanding becomes a little clearer. It is my true hope that the reality of God will be known in this world, a little bit at a time through His light as it shines through me.

Born Again?

For once you were darkness, but now in the Lord you are
light. Live as children of light. (Ephesians 5:8, NRSV)

As a parish pastor, I had numerous opportunities to lead Bible studies.
One morning I was leading a Bible Study during Lent as we prepared
our hearts to remember the crucifixion and resurrection of Jesus. We
began our time of study with a series of questions which reflected the
readings from worship the day before. Fortunately I had preached
the day before, which meant that I had done extensive research
recently into this piece of Scripture. But today was a different day,
and God had a new message for me, one that I will never forget!

With each question asked we were to share our thoughts as we felt
led. All of a sudden I became very anxious, fearful, and emotional.
Our first question asked us to list three things we had been told
about our birth. Most people shared things like the weather, day of
the week, or something significant that took place in history at that
time. For me this question was very difficult. Part of me wanted to
flee the room, but since I was the leader and had just preached in
worship, I was seen as the expert for the moment and couldn't just
quietly slip out of the room. I began to ask myself, "Why is this so
difficult? Why is my heart racing? Why did the darkness of this
text envelop me?" I sat in a room of caring Christians who knew a
bit of my life story, but the darkness was so vivid it overwhelmed
me. I froze as the tears flowed down my cheeks.

8

Somehow I was able to control my emotions for the moment as we continued to discuss the Gospel text, a text I'd read hundreds of times in my life. Once again the words of John 3:1-17 were read aloud. This is a story of the rich man named Nicodemus, who went to Jesus by night and learned about being born again, or born of Jesus.

Now there was a man of the Pharisees named Nicodemus, a member of the Jewish ruling council. He came to Jesus at night and said, "Rabbi, we know you are a teacher who has come from God. For no one could perform the miraculous signs you are doing if God were not with him."

In reply Jesus declared, "I tell you the truth, no one can see the kingdom of God unless he is born again."

"How can a man be born when he is old?" Nicodemus asked. "Surely he cannot enter a second time into his mother's womb to be born!"

Jesus answered, "I tell you the truth, no one can enter the kingdom of God unless he is born of water and the Spirit. Flesh gives birth to flesh, but the Spirit gives birth to spirit. You should not be surprised at my saying, 'You must be born again.' The wind blows wherever it pleases. You hear its sound, but you cannot tell where it comes from or where it is going. So it is with everyone born of the Spirit."

"How can this be?" Nicodemus asked.

"You are Israel's teacher," said Jesus, "and do you not understand these things? I tell you the truth, we speak of what we know, and we testify to what we have seen, but still you do not accept our testimony. I have spoken to you of earthly things and you do not believe; how then will you believe if I speak of heavenly things? No one has ever gone into heaven except the one who came from heaven—the Son of Man. Just as Moses lifted up the snake in the desert, so the Son of Man must be lifted up, that everyone who believes in him may have eternal life."

For God so loved the world that he gave his one and only Son, that whoever believes in him shall not perish but have eternal life. For God did not send his Son into the world to condemn the world, but to save the world through him. (John 3:1-17, NIV)

This text can and has been analyzed and criticized in many ways. I had previously read and studied this text many times throughout my life, but this time I was deeply moved. This time, God had a clear message for me. I will never cease to be amazed at how a person can read, listen to, and study Scripture and then one day, a completely different meaning becomes vividly clear which changes our lives. This particular day, as the tears began to stream down my face and I was suddenly unable to move or speak, thoughts of my birth raced in my mind and how it was so much like this story in Scripture. I was Nicodemus! This story was about me.

You see, my birth into this world brought darkness for many: family, friends, and even those we barely knew. Similar to

Nicodemus, I came to Jesus by night, in darkness and pain. What would my future hold? What would our family life be like? How would all of our questions be answered or understood? Even if there truly were answers to the many questions being raised, would the answers bring clarity or bring to light more difficult questions? With this train of thought and the devastation of many hearts, darkness came.

When I think of darkness, I think of fear, confusion, coldness, a lack of direction, and being abandoned or alone. In all reality this describes so many of our lives at some point. The world we live in can be a very dark place. It is filled with painful experiences and people with mean-spirited intentions. This often leads us in a direction which makes things worse. These are the times when we try to fix things on our own, seclude ourselves from others, and turn our thoughts and actions inward. I don't know about you, but I am not that much fun to be around when life is messed up. Throughout Scripture, God is said to come to us in our darkest time. Interestingly enough, God wants to be near us when we cry uncontrollably. God wants to be invited into our mess and muck and clean us from the inside out. When we can't see the path that is before us and fear the next steps, God wants to be our guide.

As I entered this world and brought darkness with me, God met my family and opened a door to new life. With this new life, God brought light and a path. I have always likened this to a child's dark room. It can be a very scary place until a small item called a nightlight is used. It is when this tiny light shines that safety, comfort, hope, and the freedom to dream come into being. As God met my family, a light that was larger than life shined down on us and lit the way.

Yes, when I was born there were many questions, some of which are still not answered and may never be. What happened? Whose fault is it? How long will she live? How hard will life be? What do we dare to do? Where do we start?

To this day, I think where we started made all the difference. We looked up. We looked up to the hand and heart of God. It was there that a strong relationship with our pastor became a reminder of who God is and who God promised to be for all time. Our pastor certainly didn't have all the answers. In fact, I am pretty sure he would deny having any answers. Instead, it was his listening ear, pastoral presence, great care, and compassion that kept leading us to the feet of Jesus. We learned to go to Jesus not with just our complexities of life but with our joys as well. This turned life around because we quickly began to look deeply for the blessings and joy of this life, despite the numerous questions and frightening experiences we had to endure.

In addition to looking up and starting with God, I was brought to the waters of baptism as Scripture and our faith directed. The significance for me became that the cleansing waters of baptism invited me not only to new life but also a new birth. It was a time for the darkness of my human birth to be given to God and the light of this spiritual birth to be at the forefront of my life. That is exactly what happened. God was invited into the darkness and became my nightlight. My life and future looked so dark when seen with human eyes, yet His single light - His presence - brought comfort and hope.

The day I was baptized my mother held me in her arms at the font. We were surrounded by family, friends, a faith community, water, and the light of Christ. I was two months old and the obstacles of my life had just begun. My mother had no idea what the future would hold for her or for me. So as she stood there with me in her arms she prayed a prayer, the kind of prayer between a loving mother and God. She tearfully prayed, "Whatever you do, use my daughter." She invited the new life of Jesus Christ into the tiny child in her arms. Somehow, beyond what she could envision that morning, she believed that God would do something with my life. My mom continues to tell me about that day and how she felt when God came not only into my life but the difficult situation our entire family was struggling with. Ultimately, the day of my baptism provided the perfect opportunity for God to reveal His power and purpose for my life. Typically, it is a time to ask for blessings and peace for the new life. For me it was a time to ask God to show us the blessings and peace in the midst of the struggle.

My mom believes with all her heart that God heard her cry for help that day. The day I was baptized she became more than my mother - she became my advocate. She was the one to teach me by telling others to love me for who I am, not to look at the outside, but instead look at the inside of my heart and soul. My mom grew up in an abusive, alcoholic family and she wanted me to be filled with the things she wasn't. It was her desire for me to have high self-esteem, self-confidence, and to know there wasn't anything I couldn't do with God at my side.

This was only the beginning. This was the time when we acknowledged the true presence of God in the midst of our difficulty, a time when we gathered with our Christian family not only to lean on one another but to praise God for what was to come. Hope became not just a constant word, it became an expectation. Hope was what we expected. Hope acknowledges the difficulty of today while expecting the joy of tomorrow. Early on this became my approach to life and all that came with it.

You might be asking yourself, "So what happened at the rest of the Bible study?" I was very fortunate to have incredibly faithful followers present that day. This life changing realization for me was met by the love and understanding of others. Thankfully they encouraged me to share through my tears. Having a monumental spiritual breakthrough in the middle of a Bible study worked to my advantage. I was able to open up to those present and later to those close to me and my life's journey. What I learned that morning has transformed how I think about my birth. I went from believing my birth was something of a tragedy of darkness to a light of joy and hope, all because of my perception and willingness to look at God's Word differently.

Now, whenever skies in my life seem dark, I know that God continues to be there. And if God is there then I know something positive will come out of it. God is my nightlight, so as I journey from the darkness of this world to follow the light, God's blessings and peace will light the way. Obstacle or not, hope is always there. And with the presence of Christ, joy can always come out of pain and suffering. When the darkness overwhelms you, seek the light. It only takes a little light to make a lifetime's worth of difference.

Did I Forget to Mention That?

There are many stories I do not remember. Instead, I remember them being told to me, years after the experiences took place. I do however remember this particular story. I remember the looks on different faces and the words spoken as if it took place yesterday. This is one of my favorite stories of God's blessings. In fact the blessing was hidden for over a decade as no one knew God had blessed me, not even me.

One of the deformities I was born with involved my right hand. The tendons and ligaments directed my fingers to go in ways different than most. My middle and index fingers were very close and worked well together. In addition, my thumb pointed towards my elbow, not the direction of my other fingers. To this day, I will often pick up items with my index and middle fingers, simply because they work together better than my thumb and index finger. I wore a brace on this hand for quite some time with hope that it could be trained to work the way most people's hands work. Unfortunately the brace did not work as hoped.

When I was a little over three years old, I had surgery on my right hand. The intention of this particular surgery was to rearrange tendons and ligaments so that my hand could be of better use than it had been. After surgery I wore a cast for a while and then a brace again to train my hand to work in its new configuration. This has been the only surgery on my right hand.

I was soon out of the brace and life went on. We did not think much about the whole ordeal. Well, at least I didn't. All I really knew growing up was that my right hand was a little larger than my left, it had a few scars and it didn't work as well as my left. There is a part of my palm that has a fatty texture to it. I never think about it and often forget it is there. Sometimes when I shake hands with someone they think I am holding something strange in my hand while shaking theirs. For some reason it must feel odd for others to shake this hand. It doesn't hurt, so it is easy to forget it's there. Other than that, I used my hand like any other person might.

Since I wore a brace or cast on my right hand for the first few years of my life, it makes sense that my left hand worked better. It also makes sense that I became left handed. I have always been left handed, but when it comes to arm wrestling and throwing a ball I am much better doing this with my right hand—but that's a different story altogether. Other than the occasional left handed jokes, all was as expected, so we thought.

Life went on and I did many of the things other children did. Of course some things came along that were a bit more challenging, but I would try anyway. When I was seven years old I had the opportunity to take piano lessons from our church organist. I enjoyed music and was in the children's choir at church. This was a good addition to my life and development, and it didn't have a big impact on my physical limitations. Playing the piano was fun, especially when I was really learning and growing in this new-found talent. Over the course of my training I had many teachers. Some were definitely more fun than others, and some really pushed me hard. Early on when I went to a new teacher my parents found out quickly that I had initially learned to play mostly by ear and could not read most of the notes, especially for the left hand. That was a big oops and I obviously had a lot of learning to do.

The longer I played the more opportunities I had to play at church, in recitals, and eventually competitions. I was also trained in music theory and received certifications for my studies. My first competition was in junior high school. I had worked for at least half of the year on one piece of music, until I knew it extremely well. I must admit, there were times when I got tired of that piece of music, and I can only imagine how my parents felt, especially when they had to listen to me learn it, wrong notes and all.

Finally after months of practice, it was time for the competition. The teacher I had at the time expected all of her students to be in this competition, no matter what their skill level. I knew my music well, but compared to those I competed against, I was a rookie.

After my last lesson before the competition, my teacher told my mom privately that she was concerned that I knew my piece too well. Not only did I know the notes perfectly, but I knew how to convey what the piece said. I had the emotion and feeling for the notes that brought the piece to life. Because I had practiced the song for so many months, my teacher wasn't sure how I would perform under the stress of the competition. There were two ways it could go, and no one knew which it would be. Fortunately for me, I was not told this information.

I performed exactly as practiced, emotion and all - perfectly! The stress of the competition did not break my concentration. I played just as I did every time I played the piece. I knew I had played well, but also knew that there were numerous other students who played much more difficult pieces far better than I could dream of playing. With anticipation for what the judges said, I waited for my teacher to call me at home that night. When she called, I learned that they were very impressed with my playing and with the emotion I played with, in spite of the ease of my piece. Eventually the competition would end at the state level.

Much to my and my parent's surprise, I won my first competition and went on to the semi-finals. I remember my teacher telling my mom and me that I had won because of the emotion I brought to my piece, but she could not recall a time when a relatively "beginner" piece had ever won any level of this competition. She also wanted me to know that even if I played at the semi-finals as well as I had at the first competition, I would not win with the limited complexity of my piece. Needless to say, I was overjoyed that I had won in the first place and was excited to play in the next round of competition. Again I played perfectly, but as warned, I did not win. Those I competed against were absolutely amazing, and their long musical numbers were extremely complex. All in all, it was an incredible opportunity, and I enjoyed it.

I continued to study piano through college and minored in it. Today, I would not consider myself a great player, but I can play. I do not play by ear anymore. In fact, if I do not have music, I am completely lost. Interestingly, when I am typing at the computer, I think more clearly if music is playing. In my world, the faster or more upbeat the music playing is, the faster and more accurate my typing. Pretty awesome, huh?

With these thoughts in mind, here's the best part of the story. When I was sixteen years old, I had an appointment to see the doctor who did my surgery thirteen years earlier. To me, this seemed silly and a waste of time. Why should I go to a doctor I had not seen in over a decade, in order to tell him things are still working just fine? That afternoon the doctor appeared in my clinic room with nine medical interns. This was a teaching hospital, but I thought this was very odd. I was not even sure he would remember me.

The doctor began by asking me how things were going and then how my hand was working for me. I responded that I was doing great and that my hand was fine, although I was left handed. He responded, "I see." By that time, I was feeling pretty silly for being there. I began to wonder what more could be said? What more were we going to do? Thank goodness my mom jumped in. It had to have been divine intervention, because I would have never said anything, and I am certain the doctor would never have asked, especially in front of his students. My mom suggested I tell my doctor what I had done the weekend before. I did not see the point, but anything would be better than everyone staring at my hand in awkward silence. I then told the doctor and his nine interns that I had played in a piano recital last weekend. In addition, I told them I started playing when I was seven and had played in numerous recitals and competitions over the years. I thought my doctor was going to fall over as his mouth dropped open! Then with the words that flowed from his mouth, I thought my mom and I were going to faint. "Let me see your hand again. I've never see that surgical procedure work before!!" My mom and I were shocked. Here I had been using my hand as I thought was normal and expected for the past thirteen years and he had never seen this surgery work before!

We were certainly feeling watched over by God, the Master Healer. I had truly been blessed once again. We never expected my hand surgery to fail. We were never given any reason to doubt its success. We now know the extent of the risk that was taken thirteen years before. It is amazing what can be done when you have good doctors who are willing to take a chance on you and take a risk, hoping that they can somehow make things even just a little better.

I do not know what that doctor expected to happen during surgery that day so long ago. I believe he felt limited in his options, and even though he had never seen this particular surgical procedure work before, he felt that it would make my life better, even if only a little. God took this doctor and my tenacious mindset that things would work out, knowing that a long lost miracle would rise to the surface many years later. What joy abounds!

Did I ever know that God was working in my life as it related to my hand prior to learning the surgery had never worked before? No. Do I know today that He was? Of course, as things are almost always more clear when we look back. The use of my hand was something that I had taken for granted for many years. This has reminded me that I always have something I take for granted. So often it is important to know the whole story, but sometimes God saves the best part of the story for later. The best always comes in God's way, and most certainly in God's time. Sometimes the miracle comes right away. Sometimes it comes 13 years later, and sometimes in just three days. Only God knows what is best and what will make the right impact on the right people at the right time.

Reality Check

Reflecting on my past, I have found it helpful to speak with those who have walked alongside me through this journey of life. With each new day, I find more questions to ask. Most of the details of this story were told to me in recent years. Due to my age when everything took place, I have no memories of my own. That too is a gift from God.

On December 19, 1972 my mom found a knot in my right thigh. She took me to the doctor who decided it needed to be x-rayed so they would know what they were actually dealing with. Since I have so many different types of tumors throughout my body, there was a question as to which type of tumor had popped up this time. My family enjoyed the holiday season and at the end of January I had my thigh x-rayed a week before my next doctor's appointment. The process of meeting with doctors often meant several appointments on different days of the week. I would often have tests one day and then return later in the week when the results were in to see the doctor. The day of this x-ray was one of those busy days at the clinic when a bunch of appointments for different doctors were crammed into one intense day. This made for long hours on the road, as well as at the doctor's office. After the x-ray on my leg I saw my urologist to make sure I had healed from the surgery done on my ureters in late November of the previous year. Then I went to have the splint I wore on my right hand adjusted. We had a long wait that day, as Pat Riley from the Los Angeles Lakers was having his own splint made. Too bad at the age of three I didn't care much for basketball, let alone understand that a celebrity was in my midst. My brother probably wished he had been there that day or I had at least gotten him an autograph. Sorry big brother, if I had only known, I am sure my sweet toddler smile would have wooed him to at least sign a piece of scrap paper for me.

After all of these appointments my mom and I headed home. As usual we left during rush hour in Los Angeles. We traveled over 90 miles each direction, before several freeways were complete and connected including Interstate 5 and Highway 14. Several freeways were actually two lane roads. I remember desperately wishing we could listen to music or anything other than the traffic report on the radio during this long drive home. As an adult who has commuted to work, I now understand the need to know what the traffic situation is, but at the age of three, it was just gibberish. I was carefree and ignorant of anything being wrong, whether about traffic on the trip home or what would be around the corner for me medically-speaking.

I can only imagine what my mom thought as she drove home: a tired (and probably cranky) three-year-old sitting in the back seat, all the while her mind and heart mulling over all the things she did, heard, saw, and thought that day. Sometimes it is hard to have clarity when there are several complexities going on at the same time. Today I wonder if she thought more about whether my hand brace would finally fit this time, if my ureters were healing well or if they would require additional surgery, or what the tumor on my leg could possibly mean for our family's future. What I do know is that every time we went to the clinic or hospital, we saw other families who were much worse off than we were. We saw children who had more critical medical issues, families with more than one child who was ill, and families deep in conflict. Even though her mind may have been bouncing back and forth between the "what ifs" and the "maybes," my mom knew that no matter how critical my health ever became, our family and faith were strong. God wasn't going anywhere.

A week later, mom and I traveled back to the doctor in Los Angeles to learn what he knew now about the knot in my thigh. I was there, but in no way did I understand what the doctor said. In a sense my mom sat there alone listening anxiously to the doctor. She was told the tumor needed to be surgically removed. Of course numerous times a day throughout the world people hear that they need surgery. In any normal setting this news may have been taken with a slightly heavy heart, but for us it remained doable - we would do what needed to be done. Still, it was not what my parents had hoped to hear.

Now there were big decisions to be made. The tumor in my leg was not the only thing going on at the time. In addition to recovering from surgery on my ureters and treating my right hand initially with a splint, I also had a mass in my right lung, a growth on my neck, and a massive lipoma (a fatty tumor) on my back. So, along with the doctors, my parents had to decide what the most important, most critical medical issue I had going on then. Where should we start and how would we proceed? It ended up that the surgery for the tumor in my thigh did not take place until the end of November, after all of the more critical tests and surgeries took place. The end of November was almost a year after the tumor was first discovered.

I was admitted two days prior to surgery so that I could have additional testing done on my kidneys, ureters, and bladder before they removed the tumor from my thigh. Not unlike the days filled with doctor appointments, my hospitalizations were filled with taking care of more than one issue at a time. Yes, I was hospitalized for the surgery on my thigh, but this was also a prime time to do additional invasive procedures that would also require being hospitalized.

Before my surgery took place my parents had been provided with information regarding this particular surgery. It was described as a fairly minor surgery, comparatively speaking. That was the main reason we waited nearly a year to do it. This was a minor surgery so the other treatments and surgeries took priority. I was expected to be in the hospital only a day or two after surgery. After deep prayer and conversation, my parents decided that my mom would come by herself the day of surgery. Since we lived so far away, this meant that after I was taken to surgery, my mom sat alone to wait. When my mom learned that I was in the recovery room she returned to my room to wait for the surgeon to come speak with her.

My doctor was a pediatric surgeon specializing in masses and bone cancers. When he arrived at my room, he told my mom some unexpected news: the tumor had infiltrated the entire thigh muscle, so the muscle had to be removed along with the tumor. In addition, the tumor was malignant. The surgeon told my mom that I could go home for Christmas, but would have to return immediately after the holidays for extensive surgery on my leg followed by treatment for cancer.

He said he was sorry, but saying you are sorry does not comfort the heart of a devastated parent. So she sat alone, far from home, removed from the comfort of familiar faces awaiting my return from the recovery room. What would she say to her four year old? How would she tell her husband? Son? Pastor? Friends?

That which my parents feared each time I had a tumor removed had happened. My mom called my dad, who felt helpless and wished he was there for both of us. My dad would do anything he could for his family. I can only imagine how both of them were feeling that day. Mom had a desire to comfort her young daughter, while also wanting to break down in devastation. Dad, at work because this was a 'fairly minor surgery' now wished he had chosen to go to the hospital that day so that he could comfort his daughter and wife and also hear the information first-hand. The rational decision to stay and go to work that day hadn't gone as planned. They both questioned their hearts and my future. All the while both of them knew that there wasn't much either of them personally could do to make the situation better. Together they decided to call our church and added my name to the prayer list. This was not the first time I had been put on the prayer list, nor would it be the last.

I have asked my mom to think back on that day many times and to think about how she really felt. This has proven to be an extremely difficult task. God has erased many of those moments from her memory. She describes it as though her memory is clouded by what she knows now. She presumes she felt a sense of disbelief, sadness, and fear because now we had yet another rough road ahead. Mom thought this was the beginning of the cancerous spurs my physicians had told my parents would begin to pop up all over my body. She wondered how much more I would have to endure and if she would be strong enough to deal with what was about to come. In all reality, these feelings are similar to those she felt the day I was born.

I truthfully don't know how we made it through the holidays that year, but we did. Knowing what would be taking place as the New Year greeted us, it must have been difficult to celebrate, although the holidays are about celebrating the birth of a Savior; the birth of one who promises new life, hope, healing, and wholeness.

So as directed, my mom, dad and I returned to see the pediatric surgeon after the holidays. The doctor came in and examined me. My leg had healed quite well from the surgery. My parents were overwhelmed by the words he spoke. The doctor informed them that they do two biopsies on any mass or tumor; one at the time of surgery and a second immediately after. When the surgeon spoke to my mom while I was in the recovery room, he provided her with the initial biopsy report. A follow up biopsy was done and there was no cancer! That's right, NO CANCER!!!!

At this time my doctor let us know that I didn't need further surgery or treatment. There was a smaller tumor left in my thigh but the surgeon didn't feel it was a threat since it was much smaller than the one recently taken out. Also, with a non-malignant biopsy there was time to wait and see what this tumor would do, if anything.

The surgeon could not explain what had happened. The first biopsy showed cancer and the follow-up didn't. This was not the first time or the last that the medical profession would eat their words, give them to God, or stand in awe. There have been no further issues with my right thigh. The small tumor that we were going to wait and see what it would do, has done nothing all these years.

At the age of four, this miracle didn't mean much to me. Years later when this story was told to me, I could comprehend and absorb it, and it left me in a state of shock. I had lived all this time and never

knew there was the possibility I had cancer. I vividly remember
the surgeon who performed the surgery. I saw him for many
years in relation to other tumors. I never knew that he specialized
in pediatric masses and bone cancers. Today, I continue to be
amazed by the outcome of this miraculous story. I clearly see the
hand of God present specifically in these circumstances and in
my life in general.

The chain of events ended as it had begun: a benign tumor. As a
person a faith, I see this not as a coincidence, but as the hand of
God. God not only showed His healing power, but God provided
a humble heart to a caring surgeon who verbalized an error in
diagnosis. This only proved to be an additional opportunity for
God to intervene.

This was an experience that proved powerful for me and my
family but also extended to our church, our friends, the surgeons,
the doctors who cared for me, and the staff. God gave a new
diagnosis. A new covenant! The covenant didn't say I wouldn't
suffer additional, traumatic, or critical events. What it did say was
that God will always have a hand in my life.

What is your struggle? Where is your pain? What do you need
God to heal? Have you tried to handle a situation on your own,
afraid to let someone else hear your story or sit by your side as
you wait? Are you going to let the depth of your pain go on like
this, when there is a God who desperately wants to help you not
only find answers to your questions but find ultimate healing and
freedom?

I could look back on this event and say it was all a coincidence.
But I will not allow the world to simply tell me someone "just

messed up in the lab that day." Instead I have the privilege to share an amazing story of God's love and healing power through an unexpected event in the life of a four-year-old.

God's power is present and accessible. It is my sincere hope and prayer that you see the hand of God at work in your life as you await mighty results. It is truly time for a reality check!

Advocacy

The term "advocacy" is not an easy word to define as there are many different aspects to the word. When I consider it, I think of an advocate as a person or group that takes on a cause or issue in order to bring about change or a heightened awareness of a situation. I also think that an advocate is a person or group which protects in order to make a positive impact and provide information. In the process of being an advocate, one can be the voice of those who may not be able to speak for themselves for any number of possible reasons. Many times the advocate has a personal tie to the cause and they understand the process may not only be long but also very difficult. The deep desire for things to be different is many times what drives the actions of the advocate.

At a young age, I learned what it meant to be an advocate. I was taught by example to help others when I could, offer support, listen to others when they faced difficulty, and feel comfortable asking questions of authority figures. When my mom and I met with doctors, she requested they speak directly to me, not to her. She wanted the physicians to understand that I knew what was going on and had a right to know what the plan of care would be. Some physicians had difficulty with this process, as they were familiar with speaking to the parent and not necessarily the patient. Not only did many physicians believe I was too young to understand, they also viewed talking directly to a child as inappropriate. After all, I wouldn't be signing the consent nor would I be paying the bill. One physician in particular informed my mom that it was of no use and a waste of his time because I was too young and there was no possible way I could understand what he was describing about my upcoming surgery. In turn, my mom directed him to ask me to tell him what was going to happen. I responded using medical language mixed with that of a three year old to very accurately describe my upcoming surgery. From that moment on this physician always spoke directly to me. He realized that my parents had taught me a lot after each appointment so that I was familiar and less afraid of what would be happening to me and my body.

The Intensive Care Unit (ICU) was very different when I was a child than it is today. Patients were lined up in one large room rather than each having their own room for privacy. Often times in the ICU patients are in great pain and family visits are limited. Since I had been admitted to the hospital, had surgery, and been to the ICU several times beginning at a very young age, it was not uncommon for me to offer words of encouragement to other children to whom this was a new or frightening experience. I would remind them that they were in good hands, Jesus loved them, and their family would be able to see them soon. I offered the comforting words that I had been given by my parents. After leaving the ICU it was not uncommon for us to be in the same room or near each other for the remainder of our recovery. Some of us who had similar medical issues would see each other on different trips to the hospital and during our recovery period.

During my school age years, my mom and I had the opportunity to teach nursing students a bit about bedside manner and caring for patients and their families. The instructor at the Lutheran College near our home went to our church and felt it would be helpful to have her students hear from those who have experienced patient care first-hand. My mom and I wanted to teach these nurses how they could enhance what they learned in their nursing classes by allowing their hearts to meet their patients where they were. We shared our thoughts on nursing care and emphasized the importance of encouraging words, family support, active listening, and - perhaps most important of all - a smiling face. Thus began my desire to help guide those in the medical profession by bringing the needs of the patient to the forefront.

As I grew older the opportunities for me to advocate grew. There also came a time when I had to transition from being the child to the adult. The summer after my first year away at college proved to be one of challenge and growth. I had turned 18 since my last surgery, so this would be the first time I would legally need to sign consent forms for my surgery. I had long had a deep understanding of the potential risks that came along with any surgery where general anesthesia was administered. I had known for as long as I could remember that there were serious risks involved, including the possibility of death. When I was handed the consent for this my 25th surgery, I panicked. It was very different to see those risks in print and then sign my name, legally binding my knowledge of what could possibly take place. Fortunately, since I was still on my parent's medical insurance and they were present, I was permitted to have them sign in my place, yet again. As I learned how difficult it was to sign a medical consent, I also realized how difficult it must have been for my parents over the years to sign for each surgery or procedure I had been through.

I tried to settle down, said goodbye to my parents, and was taken to the pre-op room. I had long since taken my contact lenses out and now had to relinquish my eyeglasses. I am extremely nearsighted so this step always made me feel even more vulnerable since I could not see much of anything at this point. At this time, one of the surgical staff entered and noticed that I had not signed the consent for surgery. Again I panicked. He forced the clipboard in front of me and handed me a pen directing me to quickly sign so we could begin. As the tears flowed from my eyes, I refused. Not only had it been earlier agreed that I didn't need to sign, I couldn't read the consent without at least my eyeglasses. This employee told me to sign it anyway as it was "not that big of a deal." This irritated me and I became even more upset. I had been taught to always read a document prior to signing it, no matter what. I was not about to sign a surgery consent without being able to read it first. Unfortunately, I also knew that it was not in my best interest to head to surgery this upset. A few tears before surgery were pretty typical for me as I drifted off to sleep and the surgery began, but now I was clearly upset, again. I was agitated, crying uncontrollably, and very afraid. Behind the scenes a nurse found my mom and brought her back to my pre-op room. She became my advocate yet again, informing this person that arrangements had been made permitting my parents to sign for me. All was cleared up and I began to calm down. Fortunately for me, my mom was able to stay by my side a little longer.

Approximately fifteen minutes before surgery was to begin, my anesthesiologist for this surgery entered and asked me several questions. He noticed I had been crying and asked what had happened. I responded by telling him that I usually cry right before surgery. This doctor was aware this would be my 25th operation and angrily told me it was stupid of me to cry, as there was no reason for it. He then took a medication and injected it into my IV. I had already requested no sedating premedication so I asked what he had given me. I was ignored. My mother then asked, "What medication did you just give her?" Again there was no response. Next, my nurse asked the same question, and she too was ignored. I was then quickly taken to surgery.

The next day, my anesthesiologist came to my room. He discussed with me how concerned he and my surgeon were that I required two units of blood directly after surgery and recommended that I not have surgery again. I struggled with a response because I knew he was wrong and out of line. Due to the nature of this particular surgery my surgeon expected there to be significant blood loss. In fact he directed me prior to surgery, to donate two units of blood and my brother to donate a unit as well. That provided three units of blood for my use during or after surgery, if needed. One unit of blood was not needed.

In addition, I had lived my entire life knowing that there would probably always be more surgeries. I knew with a high degree of certainty that there would always be something that needed attention. So suggesting to an eighteen year old with numerous critical medical concerns not to have surgery in the future was inappropriate. This doctor revisited the medication he injected prior to leaving the pre-op area and informed me that it was a typical pre-medication and did not contain any sedating traits. I informed him that this information would have been very helpful for my mental and emotional state, had he simply taken the time to answer the question when asked.

This, one of my most difficult operations, clearly proved to be transitional for me from childhood to adulthood. Compiling the signing of the consent with the poor communication from the anesthesiologist, helped me decipher what my personal needs were as related to surgery as well as how I expected to be treated by those who were caring for me.

Approximately one month after this surgery, I received a survey from the President and CEO of the hospital. The survey asked general questions about my recent stay and care received. The survey concluded with an open-ended portion for me to write anything further I wanted him to know. I took this opportunity to let him know that during my stay, most of my expectations had been met very well. Unfortunately, I also let him know about the one person who interfered with the care I received. I wrote about the lack of respect not only for me and my mom, but also for his staff. I directed my concerns as a desire for improved bedside manner and concern for the person lying in the bed. He may have been a great anesthesiologist, but when a doctor chooses to not care about others, my trust in their ability rapidly declines.

A few weeks later I received a response from the Director of Patient Relations. She had spoken directly to the President and CEO regarding my letter and the concerns contained in it. In addition, she had discussed the situation extensively with the doctor in question. My comments were read, appreciated, discussed, and a change in one person's practice was highly directed. Up until this time, I thought being an advocate meant speaking for others when they are not able to themselves and bringing a heightened awareness to their situation. This experience taught me that sometimes, a person needs to be their own advocate. This time, I stood up for my beliefs and common decency. My hope was that in bringing this situation to light, it would help other patients have a better experience than I'd had.

Later that year, there was an article in our local newspaper which examined the ethics of the medical profession. I was struck by the author's words which focused on the lack of ethics among medical professionals with both their staff and patients. I wrote to this author affirming his work but also presenting a desire to be a part of the solution. With education and encouraging a change in behavior of those lacking ethics, the system can be refined and improved. There is a lot of good that comes from the work of those in the medical field. Unfortunately, the lack of ethics, poor decision making, and/or little concern for others is what gets highlighted, particularly in the media. The good is often forgotten. Although difficult, I try to make the best of difficult situations and help those lacking skill learn from those with a bit more experience. In addition, when I see excellence in ethics, care, or concern I feel it is vitally important to tell the person doing the appropriate act -- and their superiors. Public affirmation and recognition for a job well done can go a long way in refining the medical machine.

There is another advocate, and His name is Jesus. Above the desire my parents had for me to have an advocate and when appropriate, be an advocate, Jesus wrote on the pages of my heart what advocacy is truly about.

My dear children, I write this to you so that you will not sin. But if anybody does sin, we have an advocate with the Father—Jesus Christ, the Righteous One. He is the atoning sacrifice for our sins, and not only for ours but also for the sins of the whole world. (1 John 2:1-2, NIV)

Jesus encourages me to be faithful and not sin, but He also is aware that each of us will continue to sin even in our effort and desire to do only what is right. Jesus models the type of person and behavior that brings peace and love to the world. Jesus is my personal advocate and the advocate of the world.

Whether standing up for others who were unable to do so themselves, desiring change to make life easier for others, or standing up for my own needs, ultimately I did so with the hope that those who came after me wouldn't have to suffer as much as I did. This too is what Jesus did. This is advocacy.

Great Physicians

It is impossible for me to consider my life without taking time to recognize the great physicians that have added to my journey. I will admit there have been a few who were less than desirable and caused more difficulty and pain than necessary, but I only bring up the lesser quality physicians in recognition of the fact that I have had the honor and gift to be treated by some of the best in the medical field. The greatest of these went beyond the call of duty; offered care and compassion in addition to medical skill and knowledge; knew their patients were people with hopes, dreams, and feelings; and were willing to acknowledge when they were wrong or didn't have the answer. Additionally, they often took great risk and in the process were able to control symptoms or, better yet, heal. It is also vital to recognize that the majority of physicians who have treated me did not have a working diagnosis at the time, and for those that did, the plan of care was not much different. This meant that in my younger years - when most of my surgeries and treatments took place - the physicians were working blindly to some extent. These men and women were the full package: doctor and human being. I choose to separate the two not because I think that they are separate and distinct traits but because the human side of a physician is often left out as many people focus solely on the physician's skill. I do not want to make that mistake.

The greatest ones made room for casual conversation and laughter while tending to the medical matter at hand. They were also patient, empathetic, and good educators. It takes a gifted person to tackle a medical mystery while conversing with an infant or toddler as well as their anxious parents. When I ponder the early conversations and decisions, I often wonder how my physicians were able to do what they did.

For me it is imperative also to acknowledge that the health of the patient is far beyond the physician's responsibility. I have been blessed by intelligent and honest physicians and surgeons, caring nurses, accurate phlebotomists, gentle radiology technicians, kind housekeepers, conversational transporters, adaptable chefs, the kind creators of patient support devices, and the quick response of the maintenance crew. I admittedly have left out several departments which help make a hospital function well. Even though I have been a "frequent flyer" (repeatedly in and out of the hospital) my entire life and have worked in a hospital for several years, I am aware that much goes on behind the scenes that even I am unaware of. Some days it amazes me how many different vocations are necessary to make any hospital run smoothly. Each role is vitally important. If a surgeon is precise in doing his/her job but the housekeeper does not clean the patient's room with the proper cleansers, disinfectants, and protocols after the previous patient, the risk of infection and other complications immediately rise and it has nothing to do with the skill of the surgeon. The conclusion: everyone needs to do their job and do it well for the hospital to be successful and for patients to thrive.

I am not so naïve as to place all of the responsibility and success in the hands of the hospital staff. There is no doubt they have a significant role, but the patient has a job too! The patient's job is to listen, ask questions, follow the agreed upon plan, and when something is not right, speak up! This is vastly different than when you are at a restaurant and you waiver back and forth whether or not to tell your waiter that your $20.00 steak is overcooked. In such a situation, many times we choose to remain quiet and mutter to ourselves and perhaps those at our table. After all, this is just one dinner and we can choose never to return to this particular restaurant, right? But when it comes to our health, when something doesn't seem right, it is much wiser to ask, clarify, or blow the whistle, because this is far more important than a steak dinner - it is our life!

Patient assistance devices have improved dramatically since I was a child. I am not angry or bitter about such improvements. Instead, I am very thankful for the creativity of those who assisted me and those who made those difficult times better for future patients. Many things were not perfect, but those who cared for me tried to make the best of what they had in front of them. Patients have more options today than I could ever have dreamed of. Patients still try to fend off the dry mouth from medication, anesthesia, or being denied fluids due to a pending test or the magnitude of an illness. Today's patients are offered mint flavored sponges on a stick to dip in cool water and then wet their parched mouth. The only option I had was to suck on a damp wash cloth. Forty years ago it was a great option, but today's little flavored sponges are quite the improvement. In addition, having one's hair washed continues to be one of life's greatest sensations. When a patient's hair is incredibly dirty, the person's whole body feels horrible. When the opportunity arises to use shampoo and have squeaky clean hair, it feels amazing, even if the rest of the body is still pretty miserable. Once again, forty years ago my mom would dust baby powder into my hair and brush it. Again, it wasn't perfect, but it was certainly an improvement over doing nothing. Today, a creative person has devised a shower type cap containing a cleansing agent that is heated in a microwave-like unit, then placed on the patient's head and massaged. The soap washes the hair and does not need to be rinsed. One of my favorite new patient items is used to ward off being intensely cold in pre-op and recovery. It is a personal, disposable electric blanket that blows warm air on the patient at their chosen temperature. I want one for my personal use at home and work! Instead of being angry or bitter, I am able to see how these improvements came from the suggestions and complaints of patients like me. Creative people discovered new ways to improve the life of a patient by remembering the simple pleasures and basic needs of life. I may never have the opportunity to utilize the many improvements that have been made in patient care, but I remain thankful for the progress which has made the patient experience a bit more tolerable.

In short, the care of the patient is the great responsibility of countless people. The physicians and surgeons are typically the face of the hospital; while numerous other employees help ensure things run smoothly. Those who have cared for me over the years have done more than treat me medically. They have also been a source of calm for my parents, a balm for the soul, and a witness of God's presence.

My parents recall a surgery of mine when I was three years old. The surgery was well underway and they were waiting in the hospital's main lobby. Since I had numerous physicians it was not uncommon to run into another physician who did not have a role in my care at that particular time. During this time period, Dr. Brewer was my thoracic surgeon. I was placed in his care to monitor and possibly treat a mediastinal mass, located in the center of my chest. By this time, I had only seen him a few times in the clinic as the mass had only recently been discovered. While my parents waited for an update on my current surgery, Dr. Brewer noticed them in the lobby and walked over to talk to them. I often wonder what if he hadn't acknowledged them and stopped to talk and instead simply walked on by to tend to his day? I believe that God's purpose that day was for Dr. Brewer to have a conversation, however brief, with my parents. A casual conversation took place, but the words he spoke continue to stick with my parents to this day. This kind and gentle man noticed that my parents were anxious as they waited for an update on their daughter's surgery. Heeding God's ever so small voice, he chose to engage in conversation with them. He told them, "Don't worry - if God was not in the operating room directing us while operating on a little child, none of us would be able to do what we do." My parents were humbled and reassured that God remained in control and was present with me and the medical team in the operating room. Additionally, they were thankful again for the doctors taking care of me. This one moment has anchored my parents each time I have gone to surgery. As this encounter touched the hearts of my parents, I am certain that it also affected how I perceived my doctors and those who cared for me at the hospital. Even though my parents did not share this conversation with me at the time, it affected their response and how they responded each time they were told I would need another surgery. We believe that God sent Dr. Brewer to them that day to secure their focus and faith in God.

I am able to recognize that I was among the first to receive certain treatments, and for many surgeries the outcome could not have been predicted. The tumors which my body is filled with are of several types and sometimes it is difficult to know how they may respond to any given treatment, especially if the tumor in question is a combination of more than one type. What is the best way to treat this tumor? Will the tumor be permanently removed? Will the tumor come back, and if so will it return with a vengeance?

Will the projected treatment or surgery agitate the tumor, causing severe pain even though it is almost completely removed? These are only some of the questions that arose when dealing with my tumors. Unfortunately, most questions could not be answered until significant time had passed after a surgery or treatment.

I believe that when we consciously look for visual reminders of the hand of God, they often become easier to notice throughout time. God's handiwork is always present, but we are often too wrapped up in our own thoughts, problems, or complaints about life to notice. I too need reminders of what God is doing in my life to bring me back to an attitude of gratitude rather than one of complaint. Fortunately over time, I have increased my own ability to recognize God's hand at work right before my eyes.

It has been my belief, as long as I can remember, that each physician who made an impact on my life was somehow the hand of God in human form. I have thought about this for a considerable amount of time and I knowingly use the words "each physician." Most physicians made a positive impact by doing the unimaginable, trying something new, or taking great risk. Other physicians who left a more bitter taste in my mouth by causing frustration, disappointment, or unbelievable physical pain taught me something that opened my eyes to see the presence of God. I may not have seen the hand of God in anything that particular doctor said or did, but somewhere in the midst of the situation, God could be found.

When I think of Jesus, it is difficult to ignore His miracles: He healed the blind, cured the lepers, raised the dead, and made the paralyzed walk. Much of His life as told in the four Gospels speaks of the many miracles He performed during His short 33 years of life here on earth. In addition, Jesus has not been referred to as The Great Physician in jest or for no reason at all. Throughout His ministry, Jesus brought healing to the body, mind, and spirit of those with whom He came in contact and those who had only heard of Him, yet had faith.

> *Jesus went throughout Galilee, teaching in their synagogues, proclaiming the good news of the kingdom, and healing every disease and sickness among the people. (Matthew 4:23, NIV)*

When I consider the aspects of my health that have become more difficult as I have aged, I remember that I am fortunate and blessed to still be alive. Without the hand of God guiding my physicians and those caring for me, I can easily see my life going a different direction. Since birth, my doctors have needed to prioritize my medical issues. Sometimes that meant putting one issue on the back burner until another was under control, while other times it meant doing two surgeries at the same time because both were equally important. There were surgeries and treatments which were stopped midstream because they were not helpful or working out how my doctors expected, while others went so well more was able to be done than originally anticipated. I often think of some of the surgeries and treatments which were placed on the back burner decades ago and have remained there. Medicine is always filled with difficult decisions, but I see God's wisdom written everywhere. God's presence led me to receive the care I was supposed to receive. In the process, we each learned a bit more about the hand and direction of God in some of life's most difficult places, and in turn we are privileged to live out the story of The Great Physician in the ordinary lives of present day doctors and patients.

Never Alone

The next several years consisted of numerous trips to the doctor and hospital for tests, appointments, and surgeries. One year my mom drove over 10,000 miles simply for my medical- related purposes. It seemed that with each new hurdle God would find a way to shine through the situation and me. I continued to take piano lessons, sing in the school and church choirs, volunteer at church, all the while keeping pretty good grades in school. I often wonder how after missing so much school as a child, I did as well as I did in school. That too will be a mystery for all time.

I developed a relationship with God and our church that at times was difficult to understand. I loved being at church; Sunday School, Vacation Bible School, worship, youth group, summer camp, fellowship hour, and family events. You name it, I wanted to be there. In a sense I was like a sponge that had a deep desire to learn everything I could about God that I possibly could. I have always felt a sense of peace in the sacred space we call the sanctuary. There were times during my childhood that my mom would stop by church to talk to someone or drop something off and I would wander into the sanctuary to be in the sacred presence of God. I had some difficulty relating to those my age and often joined in the adult classes for deeper conversation. It makes sense to me now, because as I grew up my life dealt with life-altering circumstances that most children never experience.

I felt accepted by God even though I didn't always understand what God, Scripture, or my pastor were trying to convey to me. God's continual love and presence in my life was rooted deep within my heart from an early age. As this concept was firmly planted in me, it served me well as situations and circumstances in my life became more difficult. At a young age I became aware of the severity of my physical circumstances as well as my own mortality. Turning to a firmly-rooted belief that God not only loved me, but would never leave me, was life changing.

I was excited to start high school. My brother Mike was a junior when I began my freshman year. It was a treat to have him drive me to school because we parked in the upper classmen parking lot. He drove the family blazer which I loved because of its massive size and the memories of the many jeep trails our family had been on in this vehicle. I hoped that one day I too would drive it to school. It was also to my benefit that Mike was on the varsity track and football teams. Some of my fondest memories are wearing his practice jerseys to the games and cheering for my favorite player.

I had numerous doctor appointments the months leading up to high school. It was a time when we checked in with many doctors in a milestone type of manner. We made sure that my back was in good working order and that my scoliosis, which had been surgically corrected twice, wasn't in need of further repair. In addition, we checked my urinary tract. I have one kidney that is much larger than the other but is also withering away. After having several surgeries over the years to help my ureters work correctly my bladder tends to be quite a stage hog. My urologist called it an "angry bladder." Thankfully before school started in September, we had completed all the suggested tests and appointments with no further recommendations at that point.

My freshman year began fairly uneventfully. I made some new friends which were added to those I had known since first grade. My closest school friends were in choir with me. Not only did we spend a lot of practice time together, we ate lunch together daily, attended different activities, and gave many performances each year. Each semester our director planned recreational merit outings for us. My parents often joined as chaperones. To this day, I am not sure who the bigger kids were in our group, my parents or my friends. Needless to say, there were a lot of fun and memorable times.

Of course not everything memorable was fun. Many experiences I would rather not relive and would never wish on anyone. I had survived the first semester of my freshman year without defeat, injury, or a medical crisis. Sometimes this alone seems amazing. I did begin to fill out a bit. As many young women do, I gained weight before my figure decided where it would finally settle. I had always been described as tiny or petite. At first there was no concern, but after a time of continuing to gain weight, my mom reduced the amount of food she provided me and offered even healthier eating choices. Mom and I even had a side bet going that whoever arrived at their goal weight first, would receive $25.00 from the other person. I vividly remember the celery and carrots, fruit, and small lunches in my brown bag. Unfortunately, I also remember being hungry throughout the day and not feeling satisfied with celery and carrots. Despite our efforts I continued to gain weight. One afternoon, my mom and I got on the floor to exercise together. As I got in position to exercise, my mom watched as my belly rolled. Thankfully, mother's intuition took over, she touched my belly, and instantly knew with all her heart that I was not gaining weight because I was eating too much or exercising too little. I had only gained weight in my belly. Something was drastically wrong.

We were on our way to finding out exactly what was going on. I will never forget the day we discovered the mass. I endured several tests which either denied food and water or forced excess water into my system in order to get the best pictures possible. Going from one extreme to the other was enough to set me over the edge. Can you imagine this with an angry bladder? I had one last test to measure the mass and provide very detailed pictures. I vividly remember wishing we were on the road home, and knew I just had to get through this one last test. At the end we were able to see the pictures. My mom and I sat with the radiologist as pictures of the mass were shown to us. I remember looking at the screen wondering why the radiologist was drawing a line around my liver, the biggest thing in my abdomen. Soon I learned he was not drawing a line around my liver, he was drawing it around the mass. In amazement we learned that a huge mass had been growing in my abdomen. In a sense I was feeding the mass and not my body. No wonder I looked more like a malnourished child from Africa rather than a teenager from California.

There was no doubt the mass needed to come out. Fortunately it was determined that its removal was not an emergency. I was permitted to go back to school, with very limited physical activity. This certainly meant no more riding my bike until I recovered completely from surgery. It never occurred to me at the time, but if I fell, the mass could have burst. If the mass had burst, my life would have been seriously at risk. We made arrangements for surgery to take place during spring break. Most teens look forward to spring break for a vacation, hanging out with friends, and sleeping in. Instead I would be having surgery and spending at least a week in the hospital. I had great hopes that I would not miss too much school and shortly after spring break I would return to my classmates.

My most frightening surgery yet was about to take place. I had deep concerns that this mass was malignant even though I was assured by my surgeon that it was benign due to the characteristics it presented. I understood the science of the mass but I was also well aware that no one could be certain until they opened me up and a biopsy was done. I knew this routine but I had never had a mass quite this big before. I checked into the hospital a couple of days before surgery so we could prepare for what was to take place. Due to the nature of the mass, I was hospitalized at a different hospital. This was my only surgery that took place at this particular hospital. When we arrived, the pediatric unit of the hospital was full so I was given a private room in the maternity ward. When I was brought to my room I saw another girl close to my age dancing in the room next to me. She was alone in a large room for two patients. Instantly I asked if I could share a room with her instead of having my own room. Luckily, she was bored to tears and was so excited to have a roommate close to her own age. We spent the next several days becoming friends.

A normal part of preparing for abdominal surgery is having a very strict diet a few days before surgery. At this time in history, patients were hospitalized days before surgery in order to monitor and strongly limit their dietary intake. Ironically, my roommate was hospitalized because she was anorexic and was being force fed. What a pair we were. She didn't want to eat and I was grossly limited in what I was allowed to eat. I was amazed that she stood and danced to her walkman nearly 24 hours a day. She was always moving, even when she ate. I, on the other hand was limited to my bed most of the time. There was a lesson to be learned here. God has made each of us unique and in the uniqueness we each had different needs.

The morning of surgery arrived and as usual my parents arrived very early. This allowed time for us to talk and play a game before surgery. When my nurse informed us it was time, Mom and Dad were permitted to walk alongside my bed and join me on the elevator. When we got off on the surgical floor we said our goodbyes. I always hated this. I knew what to expect and they couldn't go with me. I had to do this alone. Only God and His angels could join me in the operating room. The recovery certainly was not going to be easy, especially since we did not know how much the mass had grown since the last films were taken. This meant there was no idea how large the incision would be or how the mass was really attached. There was added fear for the type and level of pain to expect, and this no one could anticipate. We could only wait until I woke up in the recovery room.

Mom and Dad kissed me, said they loved me and got back on the elevator to go have some breakfast. They were always kind and would not eat in front of me when my intake was limited due to tests or surgery. My gurney was parked in the hallway as my nurse went to check on my surgical suite. She came back a short time later and told me that there would be a delay. I would be staying in the hallway, by myself and no one knew how long it might be. I wondered why they didn't know this before they brought me down from my room. Why didn't they know this before they sent my parents away? I was in tears. I wanted my parents and they couldn't be there. A short time later, the sweetest woman gently stood beside me. She introduced herself, asked me lots of questions, kept me company, and distracted me until it was time for my surgery.

The delay was at least an hour. She was my angel that day. God knew I needed a visible reminder that He was right by my side, so He sent her. She was God in the flesh. I had learned she was a Patient Advocate and when things did not run smoothly she stepped in to help however she could. Today, she was the friend of a scared and lonely teenager. This is when God spoke deeply to my heart about using life experiences to make a difference in the world, no matter where you are at the time. I already knew God wanted me to work in ministry, but working in a hospital and caring for frightened and lonely people made a lot of sense. She made an impact on my future that day with her smile and gentle heart. God showed her how to change my fear and loneliness into a simple time of peaceful waiting.

When I returned to my room after being in recovery, my parents welcomed me back. The first words out of my mouth were, "Mom, you owe me $25.00!" After a bit of laughter they learned about the delay and felt horrible they had gone to eat. I was able to reassure them that I was not alone and that God had sent a special woman to stay with me. I then learned that I had a fourteen inch incision with more than 30 staples -- straight down my belly! My surgeon called it a railroad track and it really looked like one. The entire mass was removed along with a fallopian tube. The mass was attached between a fallopian tube and an ovary. Due to my age the surgeon wanted to preserve my ovary if possible, so he removed the fallopian tube instead. I learned more biology when I was told my remaining fallopian tube would do the work of two by reaching over to my other ovary every other month to transport an egg. I was only bummed that it didn't reduce the hassle of my menstrual cycle by half. The biopsy came back as everyone but me expected: it was officially benign!

I was ready to go home a week after I was admitted. My dad came alone to pick me up. It was going to be a father daughter excursion home. These types of trips were very few, as Dad was usually working when I was discharged from the hospital. Normally, I would greet him from the couch when he got home from work in the evening. This time we enjoyed the trip home, just the two of us. After we packed up all of my belongings and got me in a wheelchair, an older woman who volunteered at the hospital came to escort us out. She pushed the wheelchair as Dad walked beside me. Before we got to the elevator, Dad leaned over and kissed me on the cheek saying, "Sweetheart, I will go get the car and meet you out front." Dad sprinted to the elevator and quickly got on long before we arrived. As the elevator door closed with Dad inside, the sweet volunteer said, "You have such a sweet husband." I couldn't believe my ears. I was ready to burst with laughter but didn't want to embarrass her. She thought my dad was my husband and I had just had a baby, but couldn't bring it home yet for some reason. Remember, I was on the maternity floor. This was so funny. I couldn't wait to tell Dad when we were alone in the car. Dad and I laughed for miles and wondered if she needed her eyes checked.

I was so happy to be home. It was Holy Week and it was my personal goal to go to attend our church's Feast Day celebration services. This was my most favorite week of the church year and I did not want to miss it. Good Friday was especially meaningful for me this year as I had just had a very spiritual experience at the hospital. I was blessed with a successful surgery, a benign diagnosis, the visible presence of God, and peace in exchange for my fear. I had a new understanding of my own mortality this year. At fourteen years old, I now knew that Jesus died not only for my sins but also for my life!

My post-op appointment with the surgeon was on Good Friday, and Dad was able to take me to the appointment. I was so excited because not only was the incision healing well, but the surgeon had taken a picture of the mass he removed. The mass was held in his hands and appeared the size of a deflated basketball. The mass weighed twelve and one-quarter pounds. The best part was that he gave me the picture. When the surgeon gave us the final instructions for recovery, Dad says he thought the surgeon was going to fall over when I asked if I could get back on my bike yet. Once the surgeon recovered from my out-of-the-blue question, I was told I needed to wait a little longer, but I would be back on my bike soon.

The story behind the story begins here. Remember the summer before my freshman year? All of the tests and doctor appointments which took place to make sure everything was okay before I began high school? One of those tests was an ultrasound of my kidneys, bladder, ureters, ovaries, uterus, and fallopian tubes. My mom and I vividly remember that day and the technician. He was a young married man whose wife was very pregnant and had an appointment with her obstetrician the same time as my test. He continually glanced at his watch and left the room to take phone calls from his wife. He later began to rush my ultrasound because his wife had gone into labor. At one point during my ultrasound, he got an odd look on his face and Mom asked, "What?" He replied by moving the wand over the same area several times and saying, "Oh, it's nothing." Keep in mind, at this time in history the ultrasound technicians were only permitted to perform the scan. They were not allowed to talk about what they saw or thought they saw. In all reality, he did what he was supposed to do: say nothing. His job was to perform the scan and send a report to the ordering physician of what he saw. In addition, a radiologist would also look at the scans and describe the findings. Once the ultrasound was over, he quickly left to be with his wife for the arrival of their first child. Mom and I left for home, thinking nothing of the encounter.

A year after that ultrasound, and several months after the huge mass was removed, I returned to my urologist for my annual checkup. My doctor was beside himself. During my appointment he apologized as he read the notes from my ultrasound the year before, "Probable ovarian cyst. Follow up and different views recommended." A year prior, the technician saw the mass and made a funny look when he double and triple checked what he thought he saw. The radiologist also noted there was something that didn't belong, requesting further testing. The mass was a much smaller version of what was removed, but it was the same mass nonetheless. My urologist was out of the country when I had the original ultrasound, and when the report came in it was not given to the physician covering for him. Instead, it was placed in my file and put on the shelf until my physician laid his eyes on it one year later.

Everyone is distracted at some point in their life. Not all of us impact the livelihood of others by our vocation. Could we have sued? I am sure we could have. In all reality the mass should never have gotten as large as it did. We should have known shortly after the test was done and long before I started high school. But we didn't. Unfortunately, life doesn't always work that way. Sometimes things go the way they are supposed to, and other times they don't. Sometimes our life is in the hands of someone else and there is nothing we can do to about it.

One lesson I learned at a very young age is that life is not fair. Somehow, we have the idea that we should all have the same opportunities and experiences, be treated the same without regard to the circumstances, all the while being able to do what we want when we want to do it. Life doesn't work that way. When God began creation He provided us with a choice. Unfortunately with our choice of freedom, we often choose wrong. When we choose wrong it not only affects us but it affects others and their life in a way we usually cannot comprehend. The good news is that life may not always be fair, but God is fair. God only wants what is best for His children. If we are willing to give up the control of our own lives and allow God to step in, amazing things can happen.

I survived a small tumor growing into a massive one. At a critical moment in time God knew exactly where I was and that I needed help. It was then that He sent an angel to stay with me because no one else could. I drew closer to God, and out of those painful moments came a refined young woman at peace with the present and future, as long as God was by her side.

Thankful To Be Alive

One of the most powerful experiences of my life took place when I had the opportunity to live, work, and minister outside of my everyday circumstances. I went on a mission trip when I was a teenager. It is not uncommon for a teenager to return home after a mission trip and say their life was changed by the experience. I can't say my life was changed by this mission trip, but I can say it completely changed my perspective of life and where I lived.

When I began my junior year of high school, I had just turned sixteen years old. Our youth group from church had a history of going to Mexico each year for spring break to do mission work. For several years, the youth from my church had traveled to the same village south of Tijuana, Mexico. For one week the youth led Vacation Bible School (VBS) for the children and led an evening worship service for all who desired to attend.

There was a lot of planning, fundraising, leadership development, and studying that went into preparing for this week in Mexico. Plans began shortly after the school year began. I had known in my heart for years that I wanted to participate in this mission trip. I had traveled to Mexico with my family and I was taking my fourth year of Spanish in school. I loved helping out with VBS at our church each summer and already had a heart for participating in numerous facets of worship. Going on this trip made a lot of sense.

Initially, we began our preparations by learning about the country and community in which we would be serving. There was an opportunity for us to learn some key words and phrases in Spanish so we wouldn't be completely lost, although we quickly learned that our non-verbal communication would speak much louder than the words we would ever speak. By the end of the year plans were underway for the lessons we would teach during VBS and during evening worship. The ultimate goal was to help the people of the village know that God loved them.

It took many months to raise money for this powerful event. We not only raised money for our food and transportation, but also for all supplies and items we brought as gifts to the community. Since our youth group had been back to the same village several times, relationships had developed throughout the years. It was not uncommon for us to know what the community needed each year; clothing, non-perishable food, building supplies, and the like. Each year we would transport as many of these items as possible. We held several fundraising events throughout the school year including car washes and spaghetti dinners. Our congregation was a strong supporter of the youth and their efforts. Their financial assistance and partnership in prayer was an invaluable addition to our program. Between fundraising, donations from the congregation, my parents' help, and money I saved from babysitting and cleaning houses, I was able to pay for my trip.

We began to organize the evening worship services we would lead for the community. The community had a chapel, but worship would often take place outside while we were there. The chapel was small and it was common for members of the community to come worship with us because their children had participated in VBS, so we knew we had to be prepared to welcome all who gathered.

This year, I was selected to be one of those who gave an evening message. Since I had a fair amount of Spanish under my belt, I recruited my Spanish teacher to help, so I would not need a translator and could speak in the native tongue of the community. I was very excited. My teacher and I worked long and hard on my message of hope and joy. Our group would also teach several songs to the children. Needless to say, there were endless hours of preparation that went into this trip long before we got to Mexico, when the real work began.

As our preparations drew to a close, the day of departure quickly approached. Excitement grew and the packing began. Less than a week before we were to leave I was having lunch at school with friends from choir. Each of us was sharing what we were going to be doing over spring break. I was very excited as this was my first mission trip and I had heard so much from those who had gone on previous trips. In addition, I had taken on a large role in the preparations and leadership for this year's trip. While we were talking some of us were standing on short (2 ½ foot high) planter retention wall. In the blink of an eye dreaming about the week to follow, my left knee gave and I fell to the ground! A short time later my mom arrived at school and took me to the doctor. Initially, we didn't know what even happened. Secondly, we didn't know what would take place, as this was not a "normal" medical situation for me. So we waited for the results of the x-rays. Fortunately the pain was minimal. The doctor met with us and stated it didn't look like I had damaged my leg too much. From what I described and what he could tell with the x-rays, it appeared that I dislocated my knee. This was good news as nothing was broken. I was so happy because I only dislocated my knee. Fortunately, it had popped back into place all on its own. I was told that I would need to wear a brace for a while to give my knee added support. Then the bad news was delivered - I would first be in a cast for four weeks, upper thigh to ankle! My heart sank. The upcoming trip meant camping in a tent, sleeping bags on the ground, far from home, and in a foreign country. There was no way I would be going and I knew it. My mom didn't have to say a word.

After the cast was put on and dried we decided to stop by church on our way home. We first met with our pastor and brought him up to date. I had noticed my youth director's car in the parking lot and went back to see if he was busy. It wasn't difficult to see that something had happened as I walked in on crutches. After the initial disappointment, we began to filter through all I was responsible for so that it could be given to someone else. The last thing I wanted was for something to fall through the cracks just because I wasn't able to attend. We began brainstorming ideas and then redirected our conversation. Was I restricted in any way? Was I given any strong medications? How was my pain? Together we realized that I might still be able to go.

The only limitation placed on me from my doctor was that I couldn't bend my leg for at least four weeks, hence the cast. The cast had one limitation - it couldn't get wet. We were heading to "very dry" Mexico. All water we needed for the entire week we were bringing from California and showers weren't available for anyone. I was in no pain and my doctor had told me that since my leg was immobile with the cast, pain was not likely. This also meant that I had no additional medication to take. I quickly figured out how to get down to the ground and get back up with my leg in a straight cast - Step One - COMPLETE. We would be driving a couple of vans to Mexico and it was possible to seat me where I could have my leg straight for the entire trip - Step Two - COMPLETE. We learned from the other youth leader that the large group setting and community would have no additional limitations on me. As far as we could see, there was no reason I couldn't go - Step Three - COMPLETE.

Now, we had to convince my parents. I had absolutely no expectation that I would be going on this trip. I was so sad and felt like once again something I wanted with all of my being was being yanked out from under me because my body failed in some way or another. I desperately wanted to go, but knew in my heart it was not very likely. Prepare for the worst, hope for the best I kept telling myself! Little did I know, my parents had already done their own research and problem - solving. They saw no reason for me to stay home. I was shocked and wanted to jump up and down, but I didn't because then I would stay home for sure. So it was settled, I would keep packing, practicing my message in Spanish, and learning the songs as we were leaving in less than a week.

Not surprisingly, there were a few complexities that came from going on the trip in a full leg cast. I could get on the floor but needed a lot more room than my single sleeping bag space provided in our tent. This meant waiting until everyone was out of the way before doing something as simple as getting on the floor or standing up. I had to borrow jeans from my dad as my own pants wouldn't fit over the cast. Thank God for belts! The most complex task was going to the bathroom. This may be seen as TMI (too much information), but it was actually quite comedic once I figured it out. In order for a female to use the bathroom with a completely straight leg, the leg must be raised off the ground in front of her. In most bathrooms, this is not very complicated. It would work fine at home, church, or even a restaurant, but sorry folks, not in a porta - potty! Seriously, I couldn't shut the door. There were thousands of people at this event and I had to leave the door open. I don't think so. Fortunately, I learned on the second day that one of the porta - potty's was slightly bigger by a couple of inches and the door would close with my foot against it. The image is hilarious as I think back on it. This was the one thing we didn't think about. In all reality, I presume it never crossed our minds because I had done so much camping with my family where a bathroom and running water were not provided. This was just another week of camping.

This week in Mexico was an amazing experience for many of us. We developed friendships with each other, learned what it truly meant to serve, taught others about the depth of God's love, and worshipped in a way many of us never had before. We had been active participants in this experience from the beginning. We were responsible for almost every aspect of the event. It taught us responsibility, leadership, and compassion. As we began to pack up and head for home, we were invited to ponder how this experience affected our life or faith. As we felt led, we shared our individual thoughts and feelings.

We were met by a large number of people from our congregation upon our return. It was dark and the Maundy Thursday worship service had just ended. We gathered in a large circle in the parking lot, held hands, and prayed. The first thing I did once I got home was take a sponge bath. Remember I couldn't get in the shower yet. I had to wait longer than anyone for the delight of a warm shower. Fortunately by this time in my life, I was very familiar with sponge baths. I spent my evening talking with my mom about our adventures and all that had taken place.

A few weeks later we held a dinner and presentation to thank our congregation for their financial and prayer support for this experience. After dinner we showed pictures of the trip. The evening concluded with a few of us sharing the impact this experience had on our life or faith. Our brief stories were reviewed by our youth director earlier in the week, but when I got home from church the morning of the dinner, I knew the words on the paper were not what God wanted me to share. That morning I had attended the adult Sunday School class where a video presentation on African villages was shown. As I tied the two together in my mind I knew I exactly what God wanted me to say. Difficulty arose as we had been directed to talk for only a few minutes. I decided to take a risk and prepare what I knew God wanted me to say. When I arrived at the dinner that night, I spoke with my youth director and let him know that I needed to change what I would be saying and why. In addition, I requested to could go last, be permitted to summarize the other presentations, and take more than a few minutes to share. Permission was granted.

Others who spoke that evening, shared some favorite moments of the week which included; smiling children, games, new friendships, new songs, and being away from home. Each of these moments was special for me as well, but they were not anywhere close to where God had taken my heart. I had developed a new and deeper understanding of God and His love for me. I could now put into words what my heart had known for a long time. I had certainly been a part of a miraculous week in Mexico, but the Spirit worked so far in my heart that a deep imprint was left for the remainder of my life.

I recalled that shortly after I was born, my parents were informed that it was certain that my life would be extremely complex and to parent a child with critical medical needs would definitely not be easy. My parents were told they would have numerous difficult and sometimes harsh decisions to make on my behalf. Some of those decisions would have to be made quickly. This life is not for everyone. One physician told them that in other countries it was acceptable to put a child like me up for adoption. Adoption was not likely for a medically complex child, but there would be care from those who ran the orphanage. Another option included having the child placed in a group home setting and permit the government raise them. The most drastic and horrifying option was that some countries find it not only acceptable but almost expected that parents in a similar situation would take the child to the edge of town and leave them there to die, alone.

My week in Mexico made each of these options very visible to me. I witnessed a community where food, water, and shelter were limited and medical care was a true luxury. The drive to this tiny town was really not that far away from the doorstep of my home. We arrived after a moderate day of travel by car. By this time I'd had nearly 25 surgeries and it had never occurred to me that if I lived a little further south, I would likely not have had them. The children we played with and taught the love of Jesus to that week had probably never been to a doctor. It didn't take long for me to realize, that if I lived anywhere other than the USA, I might not be alive. This is a powerful discovery, especially for a sixteen year old. How could I be anything but thankful, even with my leg in a cast?

A flood of memories flooded my mind and my heart was overwhelmed. The simple location of where I was born really had determined whether I would live or not. This took my gratitude to a higher level. At first it pained me. Why was my life spared and others' lives weren't? I didn't want to deal with such questions, but what I had been taught about God forced me to ask the question. My personal theology had revolved around the concept that everyone deserves to live and everyone deserves to be loved. Through being loved, God's compassion would pour in. It became my hope that this discovery would empower others to reflect upon their own lives and realize how thankful they could be, including (or despite) current circumstances. It doesn't take a medically complicated life to realize that we are blessed in this country. We have privileges and opportunities that people in other countries never dream of.

As I prepared for this trip, I expected to use the gifts God had given me to spread some of God's good news. Through my love of children, music, and compassion for others I knew there was plenty I had to offer. It was in the offering of these gifts that God opened my vessel so wide that my own gratitude reached new heights. This experience didn't just change my life. The expectations I now had of me were raised as my entire perspective of life was altered. In addition, my life of simple joys was broadened.

Most people are capable of identifying what they are thankful for at any given moment: food, family, shelter, friends, a job, etc. Some will identify that they are thankful for life itself. Most times this is a narrow sense of gratitude as one cannot imagine life without food, home, family, or friends. The impact of this experience allowed my gratitude to soar when I realized I had so much more to thank God for. The list became endless. The little things in life that most take for granted became immensely more important to me. The one thing I was most grateful for had become my life. I now saw that there was much more for God to do through me. With the comprehension that life was truly a gift not taken for granted, I suddenly became thankful for the difficult things life had to offer as well. God's plan wove together the trial and the tribulation of life into one great tapestry. Without the trials, God's grace through the tribulation would not have been identified. So I waited with great expectation for what God had next for me in my life.

Now, each day when I rise and when I lie down, it is vital that I thank God. There are many moments throughout the day in which I offer my gratitude, but these are times of a more complete reflection. As my heart anticipates what will be offered in the day before me and the surprises which are around the corner, I thank God in advance for all He will allow me to be and experience, for which I feel a genuine gratitude. At the end of the day I have the opportunity to thank God for the blessings which made my day easier, the surprises which made me smile, and the expectation that more will come with each new day. The opportunity to offer thanks is endless with a keen eye, remaining focused, and with a sense of wonder. Moving forward, I focus on all that I can be thankful for and the simple joys this life has to offer. All in all, I had always been thankful to be alive, but after this experience, I became thankful for so much more.

Simple Joys

Each of us has our own reality about ourselves and others. Many times what we believe or think can end up being our own perception and not even close to reality. There are certain things I have thought of or believed about myself which may or may not have been real. When I put my thoughts, beliefs, and feelings together, sometimes what I come away with are generalizations. One particular aspect that stands out for me is how life affected me and how I responded to the difficulties which came my way. Many times over the course of my life I have wondered whether I was just a simple person. It has never taken much to make me happy. I don't look for grandiose opportunities or experiences. Material items are not important. The thrill of a roller coaster, sky diving, a hot air balloon, or helicopter ride over a waterfall are all just that: thrills. As my condition began to truly limit my activity, I came to the realization that these were fantastic but unrealistic dreams. My life would be at risk if my adventures came to life. The more I have read, learned, and prayed, I have grown to understand that I am not a simple person, but instead I have simple joys. It is quite simple (no pun intended): with very little effort, I find joy!

I can recall times in my life, past and present, where the simplest things truly made me happy. This concrete joy has set a precedent for my life. I believe when one has suffered much, joy has a greater impact than for someone who has suffered little. When a life is filled with trial and tribulation, often the tiniest things can make the biggest difference. Joy is similar to the night light or candle which brings great light to a dark place even though it is extremely small. So, when the trial is great, it doesn't take much to immerse or flood the situation with pure joy!

> *Consider it pure joy, my brothers and sisters, whenever you face trials of many kinds, because you know that the testing of your faith produces perseverance. Let perseverance finish its work so that you may be mature and complete, not lacking anything. (James 1:2-4, NIV)*

Our narcissistic world focuses inward without regard for others and we therefore have little skill knowing how to react or respond to others in need. Having learned extremely difficult lessons at a young age, I was able to form my expectations of life, others, and myself early on. There are times when I do not comprehend the selfish attitudes of others who do not know how to be thankful for the many gifts with which they have been blessed.

Through trials, I learned to fill my life with a joy that comes simultaneously from above and within. This means that joy is a gift given by God, not by another person or even myself. It comes directly from the Spirit. Pure joy is what shines through my eyes and smile as it overflows from my inner being. When this pure joy pours out in the midst of deep trials and tribulations, such that God allows me to be the vessel of this joy during these difficult times, this pure joy is made more obvious, genuine, and contagious! I have learned that if I truly want to be one who directs others to the power and love of God, then I must allow God's pure joy to shine through me, especially in the darkest of moments. I am amazed when someone comments that they sense a deep joy in me, followed by questions about why (or how) I can have such a spirit of hope in the midst of trials. Sometimes people understand that it is all about God's ability to invade my deepest places, but most do not understand what I mean and leave puzzled. If I attempt to smile and shine God's joy completely out of my own will, it is often very difficult and comes across as fake. But when I leave the inner places of myself to God and allow divine peace and joy to invade as they will, it is then and only then that pure joy is shared.

It is very important to me for others to comprehend that this divine joy isn't always a part of me. I too struggle and ask God "why?" I wonder when things will be different and if there is anything I can do to make the desires of my heart come to fruition any faster. There are many times when I find it difficult not only to smile but to trust and thank God. These are the times when I would rather hide in my room and have a pity party. I call these my Psalm moments. This is when I take on the voice of the one lamenting in Psalms and cry out to God in my pain and suffering.

The stories in this chapter share some of my most joyful moments in the middle of some of my most difficult trials. I hope that you will find a place where joy resonates and laugher is manifested.

From the beginning, my life has been lived with strong determination and a "Don't you dare tell me I can't do something" attitude or I would rise to the occasion and prove you wrong. I have always pushed the envelope and spoken up for what I believed was right while comforting others in the midst of their trials. I suppose people can learn to do these things by watching and learning from others, but I truly believe God gave me these as a gift to survive the path my life would take.

There were numerous birth defects that were visible at my birth, but my parents and physicians also knew that there were many defects that could not be seen by simply looking at me. One of the greatest concerns was the condition of my brain. Was there any damage? Would I understand words spoken to me? Would I be able to talk? Would my physical development be delayed? My mom watched in awe as I rolled over for the first time at five weeks old. I rolled from back to front and front to back. This is when the answers began to come. My parents had gathered with several others one afternoon when I was six months old. I was in my infant seat on the other side of the room, and no one was paying any attention to me. Wanting some attention, I clearly spoke for all in the room to hear, "Hi!" My mom knew at that exact moment that my brain was just fine. As my family still jokes, I haven't shut up since.

Shortly after my first birthday, I had the first of many surgeries on my left foot. This particular surgery would remove my second and third toes because they were too big and impeding how socks and shoes fit, not to mention my walking. After surgery I had to be restrained in my crib because my surgeon did not want me to bear weight on this foot immediately. The restraints were used because I could never have understood these instructions at the age of one. Remember the "don't tell me I can't do something" attitude? Well, by morning I had figured out how to remove the restraints and stand in my crib. No harm was done, but this was an early warning that I wasn't going to be held back for long by anyone or anything. Limitations were not going to be roadblocks, only a reminder that I would need to find another way.

Spending so much time in the hospital throughout my life taught me to rely on the strength God provided for me. When it was hard to look beyond that moment, the words of Scripture reminded me that God was doing it for me.

> *"For I know the plans I have for you," declares The Lord, "plans to prosper you and not to harm you, plans to give you hope and a future." (Jeremiah 29:11, NIV)*

I was reminded that my future is being prepared by the Creator, so God must be in and concerned with my present situation too. I was truly never alone.

I was known by hospital staff, other patients, and their family members as the little girl who was upbeat and happy. The one who would calm other children down, tell them it would be okay, and Jesus was with them. These conversations and encouraging words took place in outpatient waiting rooms, the surgical recovery room, ICU, and our six bed hospital room. I had a deep desire for everyone to have a friend. I wanted the children I was with to know what I knew: they were not alone and they were loved. It is too easy to forget that when you are a child, alone in the hospital, consumed with pain, and not understanding what was going on. I spoke up wherever I was to offer encouragement to those around me.

In addition to God, my family, and my friends from church and school, I had a very special friend who went everywhere with me. I never went anywhere without Raggedy Ann. Ann was my most treasured childhood companion.

I received my very first Raggedy Ann when I was an infant. She became more raggedy by the moment; threads began to wear thin, stuffing came out, and she was very dirty. My mom tried to wash her one day and put Ann's clothes on Raggedy Andy, while she was drying. I find it hard to believe my mom actually thought this was going to work, but I suppose it was worth the effort as Ann was really dirty. Needless to say, I was extremely angry and threw Andy across the room telling her "This is NOT Ann!" Sometime later my mom decided to try again and a new Ann was purchased. It took a long, long time for me to welcome a new, identical friend, but in time I did. Since I accepted this "new" Ann, she has remained in my possession.

After more than 40 years one can imagine how she looks. I have wrapped her right leg with gauze and tape as her leg is broken and stuffing is coming out. Her hard plastic eyes have teeth marks, as Ann helped me cope with excruciating pain. Her remaining hair is styled in a short, balding Mohawk. When I turned twenty, my mom made me a grown up Ann. She is larger and more mature. My grown up Ann joined me and my second Ann at college. I slept with this grown up Ann until my wedding night. Ann truly went everywhere with me. Ann went on numerous camping trips, to school in my backpack, and of course to the hospital. Ann has even gone to surgery with me. (Yes, really!) My surgeon, knowing how attached I was to Ann, said that she had the same germs I did so it made sense for her to join me all the way through surgery. I doubt the doctors and nurses kept her in my arms during surgery, but to this small child, my best friend joined me in the scariest place on earth, which for me was the operating room.

Our family went camping a lot. We often camped in places that were far off the beaten path. My family's favorite place is hidden behind Mammoth Mountain, California. We could fish in the creek, have campfires every night, sing songs, play games, go for jeep rides, and much more. One afternoon when I was about to turn four, I was bored and no one would play with me. My mom got tired of my requests and boredom complaints, so she told me to go sit down and try to tie my shoes. I was directed to come back only when I succeeded. This was a sneaky request, as she knew that four year olds do not necessarily have the dexterity to tie their own shoes, plus with my right hand deformities it would take me longer to master this task. Nonetheless, I went off by myself and less than fifteen minutes later came back having succeeded in teaching myself how to tie my own shoes. This reminded my mom that once again, deformities or not, I was able to comprehend and accomplish many things.

I continue to be amazed by the impact of the small delightful things of life. Anyone who has ever had the stomach flu or food poisoning understands the degree to which one can feel sick to their stomach. During these times certain foods can make all the difference in the world. I have experienced severe side effects of general anesthesia. In addition to intense nausea and vomiting, I would wake up with vertigo that lasted weeks. Any movement would increase my already miserable status. Whether old wives tales, tricks of the trade, or true therapeutic remedies, many of these "cures" became a part of my life. Ice chips are often given to someone to suck on slowly after surgery. The idea is to slowly introduce liquids back into the system while lightly relieving a severe dry mouth general anesthesia and other medications cause. I admit, I am an ice freak! I love the chewable ice that is more like the consistency of a snow cone. Ice is so elegantly simple and the perfect thing to bring refreshment. Today, if I am going to consume a cold beverage, it had better be COLD with a ton of ice. Otherwise, it is not worth drinking.

Many have heard about the benefits of lemon lime soda and saltine crackers. The bubbles of the soda help to settle the stomach as the crackers absorb some of the gas created during surgery. Whether because I consumed them so often due to the number of surgeries I had growing up, because they made me feel better during some of my sickest moments, or maybe just tasted good, lemon lime soda and saltine crackers are on par with my favorite, ice.

Another favorite food item when I am not feeling well is wintergreen mints. I will never forget the day they made their debut in my life. My dad came to visit me in the hospital one day after work. On this particular day, my mom stayed home. My dad arrived at my hospital room in the evening before his long drive home. He was all dressed up. My entire childhood my dad wore a suit and tie to work every day. This day was no different. After his long day at the office, he arrived at the hospital to visit his little girl dressed in his handsome suit only to find me extremely nauseous. I truly believe there is only one thing worse than being sick to your stomach, and that is being sick in front of someone, even if they love you. Not only was I embarrassed, but I really hoped I didn't get anything on him. After my nurse came in to help clean me up my dad gently reached into his pocket and pulled out a wintergreen mint and asked, "Want a mint?" Eagerly I took one and put it on my tongue. That taste will forever be etched in my mind and the taste buds of my tongue. It was cool, refreshing, and tingly, and it settled my stomach too.

It is easy to see that my mom and I spent a lot of time together. Between the long drives to the doctor or hospital, waiting for doctor appointments in the waiting room or private room, passing time during a hospital stay, or processing these difficulties of life together, we found our own way to cope and pass the time.

When I was in first or second grade I recall my mom writing in a tiny notebook, (2"x1") Roses are Red poems for me. She would write them, read, and reread them, and leave them for me to read to myself when she wasn't with me. To this day, I remember my favorite poem: Roses are red. Violets are blue. I bet you have cracker crumbs in bed with you. I smile when I recall those words which spoke of reality, endearment, and humor. This is what our relationship has always been about.

I have worn an entire array of patient gowns throughout my life. Most were a blue fabric, which was stiff and uncomfortable. They are similar to the gowns hospitals continue to use today. I learned early on to bring pajamas from home to the hospital just in case I could wear them instead of the hospital gown. Pajamas are the best for comfort. When permitted to wear my own clothes I always did. Not only were they comfortable, but they provided a slight distraction that I was in the hospital. In addition to the fabric gowns there was the introduction of paper, disposable gowns used in the clinic for appointments with the doctor. After mom and I had waited in the waiting room, sometimes for hours, we would be called back to a patient room to prepare for my doctor's visit. Appointments were rarely on time. So after a 90 mile drive, finding parking, having labs drawn and other tests done, we would wait for hours in the waiting room, and finally be called back to the examination room. Much to our disappointment, just because I was called to the exam room didn't mean the doctor would be in soon. So we waited for the doctor to arrive as I wore the hideous blue paper gown. I always thought the style of the gown looked like something they would wear on Star Trek. I even teased that I would wear something like it to prom one day. Unlike the typical fabric gowns, the paper ones were thrown in the trash after each appointment. After all, they were made of thick paper – and what a canvas those gowns became. We played hangman, tic-tac-toe, picture games, and much more. We even wrote lists of things we needed to remember, including what we wanted to talk to the doctor about. We were known to tear off a sleeve or make the gown shorter so we could keep our list, if needed. Once this became a tradition, the doctors knew how long we had waited for them simply by looking at the empty spots on the gown. This was an instant message to them of how punctual they were that day. We got very creative and found this to be a great way to pass time and continue to be joyful in a very boring, lonely, and sometimes fearful environment. Thanks be to God for paper gowns, for they were a great distraction!

Popsicles! Who doesn't love popsicles when it's hot and your mouth needs to be cooled off? At an early age, I discovered the joy of popsicles. The sweet, cold taste allows your mouth to be refreshed. When I was younger than five years of age, I was in the ICU after a long and difficult surgery. My parents had awakened very early so they could see me before I was taken to surgery, and this meant a long drive to the hospital first. They then spent the day at the hospital waiting for me to come out of recovery. Once I arrived in ICU they were able to take a quick glance at me before they headed home. I wasn't awake yet but laying their eyes on me helped them feel better before their long drive home. For those who have never waited in a hospital waiting room as a visitor, let me tell you, it is a draining experience. You can sit all day and become so exhausted. With all the emotions that move through your heart, the questions and what if's, the body becomes limp and overtired. I believe that being the care giver/parent can often be more painful than being the patient. I can only imagine what it felt like to only take a quick peek at me and not to see my eyes or hear my voice before they went home. But they did. They arrived home just before midnight and they would return to the hospital early the next morning. Once arriving home they barely had the energy to check in on my brother and then collapse into their own bed. Just as they nodded off to sleep, the phone rang. Remember, I was in ICU after a difficult surgery. I think just about everyone knows the feeling when the phone rings late at night. First we jump and then we think the worst. This was long before caller ID and my parents answered to hear the words; "this is Orthopedic Hospital, will you accept a collect call?" Their hearts sank. What had happened? After all they had only left the hospital a couple of hours ago. On the other end of the line they heard, "Hi, I'm eating a popsicle and I wanted to say I love you and good night." I understand this was one of those times when I about gave my parents a heart attack, but from my viewpoint, I was young, happy, and wanted to tell my mom and dad good night.

During one severe illness, I was in isolation. I was permitted very limited visitors and my door remained shut at all times. I am a very social person, so this was extremely difficult. It was also my birthday. Trying to picture a social little girl in isolation breaks my heart. So picture housekeeping coming to clean my room as I was hiding under the covers. The housekeeper was cleaning the bathroom when I began to sing "Happy birthday to me" as my red-haired girl puppet danced out from under the covers. The housekeeper came out of the bathroom to find a singing puppet dancing on my bed, but couldn't see me. She screamed as she ran out of my room. I never saw her again. I still laugh when I think of that day.

There have been times throughout my life when I have been more self-conscious than others. Sometimes my scars showed more than I wished, my body slants more to one side than the other, my hand felt different to others when they shook my hand causing odd looks, or the missing toes on my foot would cause great stares and faces of disgust. For many years my grandparents lived in Florida and early on we would drive to visit them. On one of the return trips home we stopped in Texas for the night. I played with another little girl who noticed my missing toes and asked, "Whatcha got down there?" Innocently I pointed to the tiny cut I got on my foot while at my grandma's house and told her all about it. I had no idea she was asking why I only had one toe on that foot. If only I could have been so wise my entire life. But children and adults can be cruel. Every time someone stared or made a mean comment I wasn't always tactful or gracious. When I am reminded of this story, I recall Jesus's invitation to us to come to Him like children. If we truly desire to be a part of God's kingdom, then we must get back to the basics we learned as children. We need to stop becoming stuck in what we think is important and instead remember what God says is important!

> *… Jesus called over a child, whom he stood in the middle of the room, and said, "I'm telling you, once and for all, that unless you return to square one and start over like children, you're not even going to get a look at the kingdom, let alone get in. Whoever becomes simple and elemental again, like this child, will rank high in God's kingdom. What's more, when you receive the childlike on my account, it's the same as receiving me." (Matthew 18:2-5, The Message)*

My feet have been the topic of conversation many times over. At the age of three I stood barefoot next to my dad and told him my feet were just like his except he had more toes. Then one summer as a teenager, I wore my dad's flip flops everywhere. We still can't figure out how I taught myself to walk in flip flops with one toe, but I did. One year my mom sent me the funniest card. On the cover were two people talking about being a part of the same family with the extra toes on their left foot and odd sense of humor. Upon opening the card, I read the words, "just kidding about the extra toes." No kidding! Toes or no toes our family has an odd sense of humor, which certainly helped us navigate when life's road became rocky.

A consistent theme throughout my life has been to offer thanks. I am still the type of person who writes thank you notes. Yes, snail mail ones. I firmly believe that it is important to say thank you. It not only helps us recognize what others have done for us, but it may actually make their day. Everyone gets excited when they get something in the mail that isn't a bill or junk mail. So taking time to say thank you can only bring joy. Offering our gratitude to God is even more important. I recall one Thanksgiving when our church had a traditional Thanksgiving Eve service. As we entered the sanctuary each person was handed a small piece of paper. Later in the service our pastor invited everyone to write down the one thing they were most thankful for that year. The emphasis was on the ONE thing. We then passed our papers to the ushers and during the prayer of thanks at the end of the service, our pastor offered each item up in prayer. Sometimes, even when things are done anonymously, it can be clear who wrote it. That night, my prayer was pretty obvious to everyone in the church. In fact, my mom apologized to our pastor after worship and requested the prayer slip I turned in. You see, I didn't put one thing on the list; instead I used both sides of the paper. That year, I was thankful for so much; "life, mom, dad, brother, doctors, that I could scratch (I was in a body cast for nine months that year), music, my voice so I could praise the Lord"... and the list went on. Today, when life seems to be too much to handle, I recall this prayer, and begin to offer thanks. Ultimately, even if things are not great in my life, I am still alive. When this is where I start my prayer the rest comes easily. If life has you down, begin with a word of gratitude - it can change everything, including your perspective on life.

There is so much that can be said about how music can touch the depths of a soul. Music has been an important and intricate part of my life since I can remember. Taking piano lessons and singing in church and school choirs, music has helped me to be more productive. I am one of those people who needs music playing regardless of what is going on. If I am sewing, reading, writing, cleaning, driving, working, or engaged in any activity whatsoever, I am happier and more in tune with what I am doing as long as music is playing. I am blessed by the music that God continues to put in my life. When I begin to think there is no way anyone can understand what trials I face each day, a song speaks not only to my heart but from within me. I continue to be amazed at how the words that come to us in music can be much more powerful than if the words were simply spoken.

MercyMe is one of my favorite bands. Their song lyrics make me think and sense the power of God. As with any musical group, some songs speak more to me than others. In fact I may hear a song for years before the true message becomes clear to me. When the true message is needed in my life God makes room for it to come through. The song *"Bring the Rain"* speaks volumes to and for me; the first few lines feel as if the songwriters were speaking for me.

All my life people have questioned how I could remain thankful and continue to praise God amidst the difficult circumstances of my life. Even though I have paused to ask God why some things have happened in my life, I never understood others' decision to withhold praise to God because of their circumstances. I have been asked many times why I am not angry at God for my life's struggles. For me, there is a realization that the goodness of this life has outweighed the difficulty. Each morning I rise, and even if I don't feel too well, I am alive. Currently I have outlived, by more than double, the life expectancy for a person with my disease. This alone calls for gratitude and praise to God. From the moment I was born until the time I die I will always be a child of God. This never changes. God will always love me and God will walk my entire life's journey with me. My gratitude always starts here, even when there seems to be nothing to say thank you for. When I begin with these thoughts, more always follows. I have learned that I often just need to get the ball rolling and start by being thankful for something and the rest naturally follows.

Have you ever heard a song that you felt was written especially for you? As each word is sung, your story is told. One day while driving I heard the chorus of an amazing song. I had to pull off the road to cry. These words were a part of my life. The only problem was, I didn't know the song's title or who sang it. Since that day I have not heard it on the radio again. I searched for years with no luck. One day, several years later, a parishioner of mine thought she had found the song I had been searching for. She was right. I sat and listened to every word, as if I knew exactly what would be sung next. It truly was the beginning of my life in song. The song, *"You're Beautiful"* is written by songwriters Bob Carlisle, Robert Mason Carlisle, Dennis Patton, and Russ Lee.

The words of this song allow me to picture the day I was born and how my father responded to the devastating news he heard. All the while God gave him the heart and eyes to see beauty in what God had given him in me. Despite the defects of my body and the questions flooding his mind, God began our life together with grace beyond beauty. That song became a gift I gave to my dad, which connected us in a new way. We sat together in my car as I played the CD for him. Oceans of tears flowed from both of us. No words needed to be spoken by either of us. We clung to each other and knew that God had given us to each other for a special purpose and relationship.

We each need to figure out for ourselves what our life is all about. No two stories can be the same. The circumstances which take place throughout our lives certainly make for part of the story, but how we respond to those circumstances may be more important than what actually happens to us or around us. I have found that I need to be simple. When one is surrounded by four sterile walls and movement is limited, one has to get creative. God has proven to me time and time again that there is always something to be thankful for and there is always something to bring me joy. The answer is God. My gratitude begins with God and my joy comes from God. Both are true gifts which will never be taken away.

Pastoral Presence

By this time you should have a general idea that God, faith, and my local congregation are a big part of my story. Together they laid a strong foundation for how I would understand and process the many trials which took place in my life. The church my family attended before I was born was pastored by a man who had a deep impact on my life. In my faith tradition, pastors are called by congregations who desire to be served by a particular pastor. It was early on in Pastor Johnson's career that my family met him and his family. Prior to my birth our families enjoyed each other's company and the children played together. After my birth, Pastor Johnson sat with my parents many times as they walked the "child with multiple medical needs" journey. When I was not yet five years old, Pastor Johnson was called to serve another congregation. I do not remember whether I understood what this meant -- only that some friends of ours were moving and we would not be seeing them.

A couple of years later my family also moved, as my dad was transferred to manage a different branch of the bank that employed him. This move meant a reduction in mileage traveled to doctor appointments for me as well as adding multiple freeway options to travel. The house our family moved into was in very close proximity to a church in our denomination. As a family we walked to church each Sunday, weather permitting. (Living in Southern California, the weather usually permitted our walking to church). I recall walking side by side with my brother, our parents doing the same in front of us. Each week, I followed as my parents held hands. This church would become our church home for many years to come. Interestingly, not too long after we joined this church there was a search for a new pastor. After the leaders of our church completed the interview process, they recommended a pastor to the congregation for approval: Pastor Johnson. God definitely intervened.

God knew what the future would hold. Knowing what I would endure, I believe God's desire was for this special pastor to have an important role in what I heard and learned as I responded to life. My childlike nature was happy, energetic, and inquisitive. I was met by his knowledge, quiet inspiration, and continual trust in God's powerful presence. I looked up to this man from a very young age. Not only did I admire how he led our congregation in worship but how he preached in a manner that young and old could take something away and find meaning in life. Pastor Johnson had the responsibility to teach the adults, but always seemed to have time to join the children during Sunday School, Vacation Bible School, and the Preschool our church began as a community outreach. I was amazed at his great capacity to remember people's names. When he spoke to children he always used their name. I can remember him speaking to me at a young age and saying, "Now Kristine, what do you think? What do you believe?" He did so not because he had to, but because his heart truly wanted to know.

As I grew and had a desire to be more involved in our congregation, it meant that I would have more opportunities to be in my pastor's presence and learn from him. The next 20+ years included his providing instruction and officiating at my First Communion,

Confirmation, wedding, and presenting me for Ordination. Remember, he also baptized me when I was two months old. When I look at the key stepping stones of my faith journey, Pastor Johnson has been present for each one of mine. Since my ordination, I have hinted that the only remaining step of faith for him is to officiate at my funeral. The influence he had on my faith and life development made a deep impact on who I am today as a person and a pastor.

The experiences we had in my home congregation led me to where I am today. I took classes to learn more about Holy Communion and its purpose for my life. I took away a deep connection to this sacrament and the magnitude of God's personal love for me in the painful rejection, brutal death, and glorious resurrection of His son, Jesus. Soon I was able to assist Pastor Johnson during worship as an acolyte, by lighting candles, presenting the offering to God that the congregation had given during worship, picking up the glasses used during communion, holding his worship book during baptisms, and anything else he might think of or need. This role provided an up-close view to what he did. As an acolyte I sat next to him during worship at the front of the sanctuary. While he preached I sat two feet to his right, listening and watching intently.

I will never forget my first day as an acolyte. At this time in my life, I had a true fear of fire. I couldn't even bring myself to light a match. Fortunately Pastor Johnson was patient with me. On a typical Sunday morning the acolyte and pastor prepared for worship in what we call the sacristy. Each of us would put on our robe and then pray for the worship service and the people who were present. There was a small tin with numerous matchbooks. It was the acolyte's responsibility after prayer, to take a match, light it and then light the taper of the candle lighter. With my fear of matches, I asked Pastor Johnson if he would light the taper for me. I quickly chose a book of matches and handed it to him. He responded, "Kristine, I don't think this is going to work." At first I thought he meant if I couldn't light a match maybe I shouldn't be an acolyte. Pastor Johnson handed the matchbook back to me as I thought he was instructing me to light the taper. Frightened and disappointed, I opened the matchbook only to reveal it was not a matchbook at all, but a compact sewing kit. We both laughed and found a match so we could get the service started. Pastor Johnson lit my taper and headed into the sanctuary ahead of me from the front side door. After he entered the sanctuary, I was to stay outside for a few moments. Just as I opened the door to join him, the wind blew out my taper. We both laughed again as he and I both knew I couldn't relight my taper. I fetched another match and he again came to my rescue. We survived the service and I took many additional opportunities to acolyte and assist Pastor Johnson. I loved being involved in all aspects of our church life, so whatever I could do, I did. Pastor Johnson was there with his quiet disposition and caring patience.

As a young girl, I recall Pastor Johnson making the long drive to the hospital just to visit me. I do not know how many times he did this, but it was enough to make a big impact on my life. He has always spoken to me as if I were a person with much to say and much to learn. I was never treated like a child, only a child of God. When I found life too difficult to deal with he was there to listen, let me cry, and remind me of how much God loved me just the way I was. This was truly one of my life's greatest privileges.

I recall one the greatest teaching moments Pastor Johnson had with my Confirmation class. I was thankful to share how this impacted me and my faith walk at his retirement celebration many years ago. In our church, youth who were in junior high attended Confirmation classes. These classes were to provide intensive education about our church, Lutheran history, and what made us different from other religions and Christian denominations. These classes usually took place after school. At the end of the two-and-a-half years of education each of us was given the opportunity to affirm what we believed - usually what our parents had already promised for us at our baptism. On a hot spring afternoon Pastor Johnson met with my class. Interestingly, this class was made up of the children of the leaders in our congregation. Parents of our class were professors from our nearby Lutheran college, president of the church, a former pastor of the congregation, Sunday School Superintendents, committee members, and teachers. A lot was expected from this class, but we were pretty squirrely that afternoon. Pastor Johnson made the girls sit on the opposite side of the table from the boys. Back and forth the teasing went on, and when Pastor Johnson turned around, we quickly pretended to be listening. Some of the boys had brought small squirt guns to class that day. As Pastor Johnson walked by they would strategically shoot water at the girls. Of course we squealed, whined, and tattled. Unfortunately, on one attempt to get the girls wet, the boys missed and caught Pastor Johnson. Now the teacher was wet! He scolded us and informed us that we were to wait in the classroom while he went back to his office to call each of our parents. He was so serious and I had never heard him raise his voice before. Each of us knew we were in big trouble. Our parents expected a lot of us, and with their positions in the church and community we were making them look bad too. Pastor Johnson was gone a very long time. We were certain this was not going to be an easy afternoon or evening for any of us. I half-expected our parents to walk back to the classroom with him. They did not.

You may be wondering what lesson we were taught that day. Pastor Johnson didn't call our parents. He went for a long walk instead. This gave him time to think, pray, and decide what to do next. When he returned, he gently spoke and told us he was not angry. Instead, he had walked a mile to our local Thrifty's Ice Cream store and bought each of us ice cream. At first I was so puzzled by his response. Then I realized he wanted us to learn about grace and love. He wanted us to know he loved us and wanted to give us another chance, just as Jesus did. That day, Pastor Johnson truly was the hands and feet of Jesus, even to a wild group of teenagers.

Pastor Johnson was always there for prayer or conversation. My mom and I would often stop by church on our way home from medical appointments, especially the difficult ones. My mom would talk with her friend who worked in the front office and I would walk down the hall to his office. My mom and I each needed support and encouragement beyond what we could provide each other, and church was the best place to find it.

In the quietness of his manner, Pastor Johnson never convinced me or directed me to work in the ministry. He simply answered questions when I asked and supported my decisions. It was a true gift that he officiated at my wedding. Bill and I planned our marriage service to include a formal worship service surrounding our vows. This included all formal aspects of worship including communion. Pastor Johnson stated during his message that day, "It would take a 26 page bulletin and four clergy (three groomsmen were clergy) to marry two seminarians." Everyone laughed and Bill and I knew we wanted to have this opportunity to thank God for our new life together with those closest to us. Our life purpose was to worship God, so it made sense to begin our married life with a full worship service.

As seminary drew to a close, Pastor Johnson ventured to Berkeley, California to attend my seminary graduation ceremony. This seminary was also his alma mater. Our school has a tradition of inviting family and friends to place the graduate's academic hood around the neck. Pastor Johnson joined my family in this act. Approximately six months later, Pastor Johnson was called on again, this time to present me for ordination. In many ways, his ministry came full circle that day. He had retired from formal ministry but took this precious opportunity to walk with me side by side to the formal commencement of my ministry as pastor. At the appropriate time, he presented me to our bishop and placed the beautiful red stole my mom had made over my shoulders.

Pastor Johnson was there when my life as a child of God began. Over the years he taught me what it meant to have a compassionate and giving heart. Through his words and actions he guided me closer to God and encouraged me to hold on to my faith by remaining strong in the Spirit, especially during the difficult times of my life. Pastor Johnson knew there would be many difficult times to come. Instead of teaching me to worry about them or run away in fear, he taught me a more important lesson: when life gets difficult, take time and listen to what God is saying directly to me, and never forget that God is always with me!

Pastor Johnson has always spoken with clarity, intelligence, compassion, and the Spirit within him. Putting those qualities together created a package of quiet compassion and generosity. He has been my pastor, mentor, and friend. In his quiet and gentle manner he would most likely deflect these compliments from himself and redirect them to God. God placed this man in my life for a very special purpose - while he was being the hands and feet of Jesus, he was also teaching me to do the same. I am thankful and amazed to have had such a Spirit-filled pastor who was not afraid to lead others to Jesus. Everyone needs a person like this in their life. Who is your compassionate companion? Who is your teacher? Who encourages you? Who brought Jesus to life for you?

Although these are very important questions, there are more. Who sees you as compassionate? Their teacher? Their encourager? Who did you bring to Jesus? My deepest gratitude and heartfelt thanks is given to God for placing Pastor Larry H.T. Johnson in my life; my pastor, mentor, and friend in this world and the next!

A Mani or a Pedi?

The one critical factor in every college student's life is: who will my roommate be? Throughout my five years of undergraduate college I had four roommates chosen for me by someone in administration who puts students in rooms together (based upon who knows what - for all I know they could throw darts at a wall with our pictures on it hoping for a decent match).

The four roommates that were chosen for me came from backgrounds very different than mine. It wasn't necessarily their backgrounds that made it so difficult as it was the way they treated others. It wasn't until my junior year that I was able to decide for myself who I would room with, and not all of those decisions were great either. If nothing else, it provides an example of the choices we have in life, and the opportunities we have to cooperate and learn to accommodate others - or not, as the case may be. Overall, I learned that the deal-breaker for me came down to values, not background.

One of my roommates was a friend of a friend. I didn't know her well but we did sing in the college choir together. We were going to room together the year after our choir toured London and Wales. We were fortunate enough to be roommates while in London too. It was then that we became very close and I gained a friend who would teach me much, even when I wasn't in her presence. She became more than a friend to me, she became an inspiration.

Dana had a way with humor that can make just about anyone laugh in almost every situation, good or bad. She was hard working and dedicated to all she committed herself to. Dana was one of those people you meet who takes on more than anyone else and succeeds beyond expectation, and her personal expectations were not just high, they were to be the best! Dana gave her all to her family, friends, school work, and various clubs she was a part of throughout her life.

When I met Dana, I did not know that she had a disease called Lupus. Lupus is an autoimmune disease, which means that instead of just attacking foreign substances, such as bacteria and viruses, the immune system also attacks healthy tissue. This leads to inflammation and damage to various parts of the body, including the joints, skin, kidneys, heart, lungs, blood vessels, and brain. This meant many trips to the doctor, hospitalizations, chemotherapy, and so much more.

Dana and I connected quite quickly. But for the most part we didn't talk about our medical issues. We talked about how to be uplifting to those around us and help them be more comfortable with everyday difficulties. When Dana and I were roommates in London she was still undergoing chemotherapy. So instead of forgoing an amazing trip or abandoning her health program, Dana received medical attention including chemotherapy in a foreign country. I was amazed at her trust and enthusiasm for this particular trip that allowed her illness to be shadowed by her excitement.

I do not want people to be alone if they don't want to be, but I also recognize that there is a time for people to be alone. Through our conversations I learned that Dana did not like others to be put out or inconvenienced because of her medical needs, so she would handle them alone. When she made a trip across London for chemotherapy, I was concerned that she might not feel well and may have difficulty getting back to our flat via the underground railway system. Dana, having a lot of pride, would not let me accompany her, but finally did allow me to meet her after her infusion just so she got back safely. We didn't talk about it, we just did it.

We then had the opportunity to room together for five more quarters of college. During the year that followed London, Dana would have chemotherapy once a month and of course she would drive herself to and from. I understood this sense of independence. When you have no control over something like an illness, you take control of what you can, and this was one thing Dana could control. Once back to the apartment she would endure the common side effects of chemotherapy: nausea, vomiting, weakness, and then study at the same time. Even though she put on a good front and drove herself knowing she was not going to feel well after, she did so month after month. My intuition told me that she needed to do this alone, but she also wanted someone there. This is where compromise came in. I knew which weeks Dana had chemo, what time she left for class and when she came back for her car. Each "chemotherapy Friday" throughout the year I left a 'thinking of you' note on her windshield.

You never know the impact someone will have on your life. You never know what small act of kindness will mean for someone during their day. Something that might seem almost insignificant to you might help save another's life. Sixteen years later I learned that Dana always knew she was never alone, but those notes reminded her that someone was thinking of her at that exact moment. Dana had kept those notes to provide encouragement throughout life's difficult times to come.

That year we were roommates, Dana still kept all of us laughing. One day she was reading our local paper which was advertising a special on pedicures, 10% off. Until that day, I had never thought of having a pedicure. Dana blurted out, "Kris, I wonder if they'd give you 50% off (the offered 10% plus 10% off for each toe I was missing). We were all laughing hysterically. You can't say things like this with just anyone. Before the age of three those toes were removed due to their large size and poor effect on my walking. My family and I had made jokes about my feet for years but this one really topped them all. I thought wearing flip-flops was my greatest feat—no pun intended---well maybe so! To this day, when I paint my toenails I remember this encounter with humor and the strange configurations of my body.

Since college, Dana was a bridesmaid in my wedding, came to my graduation from seminary, and attended my ordination. We did not talk very often but when we did it was as if no time had passed. Dana married several years after I did and she and her husband decided to adopt two beautiful daughters from their native China. The stories are as beautiful as the girls. They adopted their youngest in early March of 2008 and later that year, after sixteen years in remission, her lupus became active again. Playing cards one night with my husband, the phone rang. Dana had died due to complications of her Lupus. The tears flowed.

I cried in sadness for her family. I also cried because I had been so tempted over the years, especially at that particular time in my life, to forget the laughter Dana brought in the midst of difficulty.

I grew up in a family that joked and did silly things when life was tough. Why had I forgotten to continue those habits?

In light of her death there was a personal challenge to make sure that I never forget to laugh at myself. I also have put on my bucket list 'get a pedicure!'

So ... if I had the choice for a mani or a pedi, I would have to say ... pedi! Of course it will be in her honor and yes, I will ask for my 40% discount!

Kris picks flowers from the garden for her mom.

Kris and her brother Mike share a popsicle.

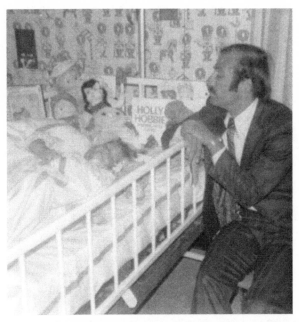

Kris's dad visits her in the hospital on her seventh birthday.

Kris in her body cast after her first spinal fusion.

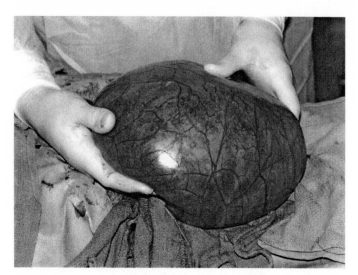

The 12.25 pound tumor removed from Kris's abdomen.

Kris and her mentor, Rev. Larry Johnson.

Kris and her niece, Hailey, on Hailey's First Communion Day.

Tara, Doug and Amy dress up for their
church Trunk or Treat event.

Kris and her mom celebrate a special birthday.

Kris and her husband Bill, find great
joy on a rainy graduation day.

You'll Be Bitter Too!

I would describe myself as a bubbly, positive, and caring person. I make great effort to take time for others and listen to what is going on in their life. I really never had anyone question my motives or why I cared before. The only aspect of my personality or character that had ever been questioned was "how can you be so upbeat when you have had so many bad things happen to you?" So when I was hit square between the eyes with the words, "when you are my age you'll be bitter too," I was shocked!

I not only knew this would not be true, but it gave me the courage and strength to make sure it did not happen, even in the midst of more trials and disappointments. This made me dedicate the rest of my life to NEVER being bitter about life and its circumstances!

When I was about to finish my fifth year of college, I struggled with what God wanted me to do with my life. I had a passion for church ministry and had experience in Christian Education and Children's Ministry, but my heart also drew me to use my medical experiences to make others' difficult situations easier. As graduation drew near, the less I knew about my career choice and the more confused I became. What I did know was that I did not want to go directly to seminary, especially for another four years of education.

It was Easter Sunday, following the family meal at my boyfriend's home when the future began to become clear, in spite of my protests. My boyfriend's parents had "adopted" me through a college program at church four years prior. I felt very close to this family. After Easter dinner, a copy of our denomination's magazine, *The Lutheran*, was placed in front of me. It was opened to the want ad section. The largest congregation in the synod to our north was looking for a full-time Youth and Christian Education Director. My boyfriend and his parents told me I needed to apply because it was perfect for me. I protested yet again! There was no way I was going to work in a church! Not now!

The more I protested, the more they insisted that I should at least apply for the job. After all, in college we were taught to apply for jobs we didn't want too, so that we could get interview experience. So I applied. I heard nothing from the church for quite some time. The funny thing was, the longer I waited to hear a response, the more I wanted the opportunity to interview.

The morning of graduation, I received a phone call asking me to come and interview. I was thrilled. A time was set for me to meet the congregation and staff, and then be interviewed by the search committee. The more involved I got in the process, the more I wanted this job! Strange how things turned around so quickly!

A short time later I was offered the job and accepted it. This was a difficult time for me, because I still had friends who were in school, a job I loved, and family who lived closer to me. I would be moving more than four hours away from everything I knew. Even though this was a job meant for me, it also meant giving up so many things that gave me a sense of safety, comfort, and love. Ironically - or should I say led by the Spirit - my parents moved from the home I grew up in to a town several hours closer to my new home.

I found myself venturing off and, for the first time in my life, living by myself. Fortunately I had help finding a place to live, since I wanted a safe neighborhood. On my own I am not sure I would have found my little area of the world, called the "Pocket Area." Quaint, quiet, bike paths with easy access, and similar to the neighborhoods in which I grew up – it was perfect. What fun my mom and I had searching for furniture to fill my apartment at garage sales. I will never forget my $25 coffee table and $35 sectional sofa. Unfortunately the smaller than normal sectional sofa was the only option for house guests. Thinking back, it was probably a good thing I didn't have overnight guests very often.

My job entailed many different tasks and, due to the timing of weekend needs, my general work hours were not what one would call normal. I worked most weekdays but found that my schedule was flexible because I had numerous weekend and evening responsibilities. Since the job I previously held was similar with regard to organizing the children and youth programs, I had a general idea of what to do. This new position now entailed providing for adult education and leading many more children and youth.

I quickly learned that I was the youngest person on staff, which isn't hard to imagine since most youth directors are college age or right out of college. I had worked on a staff before in which I was the youngest. I always tended to get along with people older than myself anyway. I love being with people in general but those who were either much older or much younger had a special place in my heart. I never thought being young was a problem. I was taught to be kind to others and simply be myself regardless of age, or any other differentiating factor.

A short time after I began this job, I learned that there was great tension among the staff. Since I was still an outsider, this meant many doors were locked tight. I was able to sense the difficulty when others seemed blind to it, probably because I was an outsider. After a few conversations I learned that the staff felt overworked, undervalued, not listened to, and for the most part were just "doing their time" until they could afford to go elsewhere. These feelings of frustration seeped into all working relationships. Staff members began not to trust anyone, including each other. I watched the staff become unproductive and angry in a very short time. Promises were made and broken over and over again, which did not create a cohesive or safe environment for anyone. Unfortunately, since I was the new kid on the block, no one trusted me or what I had to say.

The most vivid memory I have of my time there was when I was trying very hard to empathize, listen, and understand the staff perspective. I was told that it was simply a part of life to be angry, malicious, skeptical, resentful, and bitter. In addition, I was told that by the time I was their age I would be bitter too! I truly didn't understand. This was the church. This was a place in which God's Word was shared, leaders were to radiate God's love so others would want to learn more and be more like Christ. I was told I would understand this when I became their age. Being bitter was a part of life because life was so difficult and people had no other choice than to respond with a negative attitude.

Now that I am at least the age of the other employees I worked with so many years ago, I see a glimpse of why I was told what I was. I have met more people than I ever thought possible who seemingly strive to hurt others by their words and deeds. I have experienced how bitterness and the lack of understanding can tear down relationships that were once very strong. I have watched the faith of people destroyed by the circumstances of life. All the while, though, I still fundamentally disagree ... and I still don't understand. Here is what I believe: no matter what happens, we have the fortitude to move forward in life. There is nothing to be gained by sitting stagnant, angry, and bitter, waiting for life and others to apologize or pay me back.

The true reality of life is that there will always be good days and bad. You will meet people who are kind and those who care only for themselves, so much so that calling them narcissistic doesn't seem to come close. Each person has a journey to travel. Each of us must decide how it is that we wish to respond to situations and others we encounter on our journey. Do you wish to respond with a negative, closed heart focused solely on what you believe you are entitled to? Do you respond with eyes that are closed completely to the beauty each new day offers? Do you find that life is best spent in anger, complacency, and bitterness?

If you wish to travel the twists and turns of life free from all difficulty, I am not sure where to direct you. Everyone I've ever met is dealing with some difficulty. Regardless of how or when the difficulty shows up, how will you respond? I invite you to choose the response to life that says, "I will not become angry because things do not go my way. I will not turn away from those whom I trust the most because of a misunderstanding. I will not be bitter about life and my journey because it is not fair, the way I had planned, or what I've always dreamed."

Close to a year after I had started this job I made the decision to head to seminary and continue my journey toward ordained ministry. Many different situations came together that led me to make this decision, but ultimately it was God who told me I needed to go, and to go right then. Why, I did not know, but God was specific that NOW was the time. I have a vivid memory of the conversation I had with the senior pastor, who was my boss, about my decision. He asked if they, the congregation, had an impact upon my decision to go to seminary. He beamed when he asked with a smile as big as the sky. He wanted me to say that they were so wonderful that I had to be a part of congregational ministry as my career. I hesitated as I searched for the right words. The congregation was not part of the when or why I would go to seminary. I told him the most helpful information they provided me with was that the idealism I had witnessed growing up in the church is not reality. Learning that churches are not ideal and that they are as flawed as the people who make them up was how I would approach the next journey in my life.

Amazingly, it was not far into the future that I would be faced with a similar situation. I was faced with reflecting on my upbringing and trying to describe why I was so happy and full of hope. Now mind you, I had just told my boss that I learned the church was not as ideal as I once thought it was. Now I was faced with it yet again in seminary by someone who would ultimately have great influence on my career and life.

As a part of the seminary process for those wishing to be ordained, one has to go through intense psychological analysis. I spent a couple of days taking numerous tests which provided information on my IQ, personality type, verbal and cognitive thinking skills, approach to life and situations; basically, all the things that made me who I was.

After all of the tests were completed and compiled I spent a day with a psychologist reviewing, defending, and understanding my responses. The final evaluation written by the psychologist would be provided to my endorsing and approval team that would decide if it was appropriate for me to continue in the program. Needless to say, a lot of weight was placed on this review. Talk about fear. Fortunately, there was not much that surprised me from this review. I knew that my comprehension was not super and that my verbal skills were outstanding. (What does one expect from a speech major anyway?) The personality typing test I took, I had taken a few years prior in college and the results were basically the same, which the psychologist told me was to be expected. The portion of the review and evaluation that stopped me in my tracks was that the psychologist told me he thought I needed to take at least a year off of life and be angry at God for the life I was dealt. He wanted me to cry, throw things, and tell God how unfair my life was.

I was shocked! I had already missed a lot in life, why would I dream of taking time out from the experiences before me? I was judged for not being angry with God. I am usually upbeat and happy. This does not mean I never have a bad day, but I refuse to settle into a pattern of negativity because of something outside of my control. I don't believe God made me have my physical ailments, but I do believe God can make good come out of them. So why be angry at God? No matter what I said, the psychologist told me that his recommendation to my endorsement committee stood and I needed to take time away and be angry.

I was devastated. I had already moved into the dorms, made friends, started classes, and he wanted me to stop all of it to be angry, for 365 days or more. The more I thought about this, the more absurd it became. Unfortunately, I didn't meet with my endorsing committee for a few months. So I waited for the dreaded meeting with people I had never met to make a decision about my future focusing on the recommendation of one angry, bitter, and powerful man.

Once again, God prevailed. I entered the small room and was pleasantly introduced to my committee. It was led by a pastor my now-husband knew and respected. After the introductions took place, the leader informed me that the committee had read my faith statement, my career aspirations, and the recommendation of the psychologist. I did not know where the conversation would go from there, but they wanted me to know up front that they knew a lot about me and were prepared to discuss it. The following words were a shock, even to me. I had heard so many horrid stories about these endorsing committee meetings and heading in with a recommendation like the one my psychologist presented was not a good start. The leader told me that before we began my thorough evaluation they had an important question for me. He first informed me that they had carefully read the recommendation of the psychologist and then asked if I minded if they tossed his suggestion out and we simply proceeded without that portion of my packet? I am not so sure how great my verbal skills were at that moment, but I was again reminded how God can intervene and change the course, even when people try to mess things up. In some fashion I told them I didn't mind at all. I was then told they hoped I would say that because they did not want me to stop my seminary journey to ordained ministry. I had too much to offer.

Life is full of twists and turns that can rotate at any moment due to a decision by us or someone else. I have learned it is all about choices. I do not presume to suggest that there won't be days in which bitterness, anger, confusion, or loneliness consume you or me. There will be days when we honestly feel as if no one, including God, understands the circumstances we find ourselves in or surrounded by. But we must make a conscious choice on how we will take in and act on those circumstances, realizing that everyone has their own journey to travel and their own story to tell.

Do not passively sit and let the world and all its negative energy consume you – and it will if you let it. Instead, allow a flicker of light and hope to prevail. Light consumes darkness if we don't stand in the way. Let forgiveness overpower anger. In time your confusion will turn into clarity. In that moment, let joy sweeten the package we call "life" so that bitterness is not a common aftertaste. In time God will make all things new, and in their newness they will shine.

Teacher and Learner

"Teacher" and "learner" are words most come to know at a very young age. Typically children come to understand that they are the learners. They go to school to learn and the person whom they learn from is the known as the teacher. For numerous years children attend school, with hopes of making great progress each year. Expectations are placed on students and teachers by the federal government, state authorities, and local school districts along with numerous other factions. There are many different educational paths that are available to students today that I never dreamed possible when I was attending school. Sometimes it makes me laugh to know that many of today's youth have their own computer and cell phone while still in grade school, whereas I received a computer of my very own when I began my Master's Degree program and my first cell phone several years after I was married - unheard of to most youth today. In this context, however, my purpose is simple: to state that a learner is one who gains information or knowledge. A teacher is one who provides knowledge or information.

When the terms "teacher" and "learner" are broken down to their basic definitions, I am then able to see how broad the terms truly are. When I change my perspective of teacher and learner and include areas beyond the four walls of a classroom - a field trip to a museum, zoo or grocery warehouse - the teacher becomes the docent, zookeeper or grocery warehouse operations manager. The class teacher may gain knowledge alongside the young students, hence also becoming a student.

In a similar manner, let's say three children each take a trip over the summer to the same museum, zoo and grocery warehouse. When school begins in the new academic year, the same teacher assigns each student in the class the assignment to provide information on one place they visited over the summer through a verbal presentation. As each student prepares his or her own presentation, each one gains a better understanding of what they learned so that they can accurately present that information to the class. Each student continues to be a learner. In addition, when each student presents information to the class, their classmates and teacher are also learners for the moment. The student presenting now provides the information and knowledge they gained from their own personal experience. By doing so, this student now shares a role with the head of the class and becomes the teacher for this part of the educational experience.

I've come to realize that the role of teacher and learner is not cut and dry. Each of us can easily be a teacher and a learner, sometimes both at the same time. I was taught at a very young age to listen well and ask relevant, thoughtful questions. In doing so, I became a generally good learner. And because I am a good listener, I am also a good teacher. When I listen I am also able to pick up on what is said and what is not said. When I take time to listen fully I can learn a lot. I know that I only have one life on this earth and I will make more mistakes than I can count. I know I can't experience everything or know everything, so I find it amazing to live by the thoughts, questions, joys, sorrows, regrets, and experiences of others. When I ask questions and listen fervently to the answer, I have the opportunity to share in a piece of their journey.

This is one the aspects of chaplaincy that I cherish. I do not need to take the journeys others take, make their mistakes, or even agree with their thoughts, but honoring what they think, feel, or are processing at the time can be invaluable to both parties. I take to heart what others have entrusted to my care in my role as a chaplain.

When my parents taught me to ask thoughtful questions I realized that I was learning something important. I was able to add my own experience to the situation and learned that even as a young child of two or three, I had thoughts and questions about important aspects of life. This helped me paint my perspective of people and how we respond to one another. When I worked as a Youth and Family Pastor I constantly utilized these skills. I too desired for these children, no matter their age, to feel important enough to ask thoughtful and relevant questions. This meant taking time to not only teach them but to know them. In teaching the hundreds and hundreds of children and youth that I worked with over more than two decades, I needed to take time to let them teach me. Self-confidence is built when other people value us. I wanted these youth to know that I not only valued them, I also had much to learn from them. One of my guiding beliefs is that everyone is a learner AND a teacher. We may not have the title of teacher and we may not be a perpetual student, but wherever life takes us we have much to learn and much to teach.

Age has little to do with it! Size has little to do with it! Experience has little to do with it! Status and education don't either! It is all about a desire to learn and share. Most of us have heard the statement, "Our children are our future." I must admit that every time I hear those words I literally cringe. Children are not our future - they are our PRESENT! If we solely see our children as our future, we lose out on what they can teach us today. When we remind ourselves that we don't know it all, we permit ourselves to learn even as an adult. I have found that the more I open my ears and eyes to those around me, regardless of their age, education, race, experience, ability, size, or status, I learn more about life and myself. Children often know so much more than they are given credit for.

> *"Truly I tell you, anyone who will not receive the kingdom of God like a little child will never enter it."*
> *(Mark 10:15, NIV)*

Jesus tells us to come to Him like a child, and if we really look at His life, didn't He initially come to us as a child? The story of Scripture has come full circle. What better way to learn than from a child?

> *Then people brought little children to Jesus for him to place his hands on them and pray for them. But the disciples rebuked them.*
>
> *Jesus said, "Let the little children come to me, and do not hinder them, for the kingdom of heaven belongs to such as these." When he had placed his hands on them, he went on from there. (Matthew 19:13-15, NIV)*

Take a risk. Listen to a child. Open your eyes, ears, and heart to what they can teach. You will be amazed. If you aren't, perhaps you aren't as open to the suggestion as you should be.

God's Glory

Throughout scripture there are examples of people who struggle to understand God's plan and purpose. Today we struggle to comprehend why certain things happen in our lives and world. Many times we have our own ideas of how things would be better managed and question why God does the things He does instead of using our ideas. So often we believe we know everything we need to know in order to best run our own lives and the rest of the world at the same time.

Have you ever asked God, "Why?" Why are there natural disasters? Why did things turn out the way they did? Why did she die so young? Why didn't God step in and make things better and easier? There are many more questions that have been asked of God through the years. I am certain that you have asked your fair share of them, just as I have. I asked one "Why?" question of God many years ago as a young child. To be completely honest, I don't even remember asking the question, but since I have an answer I can only presume that God answered the question deep in my heart before I could even mutter the words. I believe it was God's way of helping me through my life's journey. It was a special gift from God to me that made the path a bit straighter than it had originally been.

The question was, "Why did this happen to me?" It is a simple enough question. Why, from the very beginning, was my life filled with trials? There were many trials which were obvious from the onset and others that would come up later in life. The reality was, this life would be hard, no question about that. Thus the question, "Why?"

As this question has moved in and out of my mind throughout my life, so has the answer. Most of the time the answer has been very clear but there have been a few times when life was so difficult that the true answer was quite hard to see. If I were to answer the question for myself I could be either logical or an irrational mess. Since this question was asked of God, it really doesn't matter much what I think the answer is, or what anyone else thinks the answer is for that matter. The question was to the God of the universe, so why not let God answer? When God is given the chance to answer questions, the answers are almost always very vivid. For me, when things appear that clearly as an answer from God, they are right, although sometimes it takes me a while to admit it. So when the answer is affirmed by those who know you well and/or those who barely know you, it's hard to explain it away.

So what did God say? How did God respond to my question of "Why me?" God has told me many times throughout my life that I am to teach and listen to others in response to my own trials. My trials are not in vain. When difficulties take place in our lives there are always opportunities to grow and learn. I certainly do not expect this learning or growing to take place right at that moment, although sometimes that has happened. Many times this learning takes place years later. If this opportunity to learn and grow is present, then it must be for everyone. We are not the only ones who learn from our own difficulties. Others can learn by walking the journey with us, by observing what happens, or hearing the story many years later.

God gave us each other for love, comfort, and aid. Life's difficulties seem easier when we know someone has been through what we are dealing with. We can either learn from each other or continue to make the same mistakes over and over again. I do not intend to say that each of us should live life the same as the next person, but we can learn from what others choose to do or not do. We each need to pave our own path, but if we pave it in isolation, we miss a great opportunity to learn from each other's mistakes and successes.

We are often stuck in describing things as good or bad and miss a grand explanation. Things are. Life is. We are the ones who make sense out of it. Instead of calling life's occurrences good or bad, perhaps we can strive to bring God glory out of all of it.

There was a time in my life when I learned how much faith God had in me. I had faith in God, but could it be that the Creator of the world had faith in me? I thought I was just one small person in a great big world, so how could God have faith in me? Once again, the Creator of the world proved He was not only concerned about me but had a plan that provided a purpose for His kingdom through my life. This is when God showed me the light by illuminating the error of my thinking, when I learned that what someone else has is not always good for me.

There was a time in my life when I prayed for healing, always wanting - in reality wishing - to be like everyone else. Instead, I learned that God loved me for who I was created to be. God didn't love me for trying to be like everyone else. He didn't love me for wishing that I could be them instead of being me. I was created in God's image, the apple of His eye. God knew that we could handle anything together. God knew it all along. I just needed to learn it, believe it, and learn how to live it! Once learned, I needed lots of reminding, because when things got rough, I would all-to-easily forget. God knows I need reminding, so my parents, husband, friends and the still small voice of God's spirit do just that: they remind me that I can endure anything with God's help!

I believe God allowed the things that have taken place in my life so that God could wipe the sleep from my eyes so I could see that God's gifts are all around me, even in the midst of trials. We, as humans, so desperately desire to have explanations in this life. I finally learned that the less I ask the question why, the more I understand. I know that one day I will have the answers and, for now, the answers will be revealed on a need-to-know basis.

When I look back at specific times when I truly ached for answers... when I really wondered why God had put me into a particular situation...when I wondered what it was that I needed to do to make things better...I realize that it was then that my eyes were blind, my ears were clogged, and my heart was closed. I came to God with doubts and hopelessness, and walked away hand in hand with Him. God provides the things we need that we can't envision for ourselves. He comes to us again and again to give us exactly what we need, hoping that as things change just a little, maybe this time we would see, we would understand, we would know, and we would trust.

Each of us can name things that we find difficult, the things that take our time, energy, money, and hearts. Anything that takes us away from the glory of God becomes an idol. Anything that provides an escape to look solely at ourselves is a dangerous spot to be in. So when we take the time to reflect upon our lives, do we do so with eyes that are open, ears that are ready to listen, and a heart that is ready to melt at the words of Christ as He takes us by the hand and says, "Follow me?"

When I picture Christ, I have never visualized Him as shown in those common pictures we have all seen of Jesus. The Jesus in my life doesn't come walking down the hall in sandals or barefoot. He doesn't wear a long white robe which scarcely touches the dirty ground while the long sleeves wave in the wind so He looks like an angel. He doesn't have long wavy brown hair and a neatly trimmed beard and mustache. He has two very small yet vitally important features. These are the only things that are consistent with most common pictures of Christ. As Jesus comes to me, there is always a slight smile on His face and a twinkle in His eyes. It never mattered what kind of clothing He wore. I didn't care what was on His feet or that He hadn't bathed. It didn't matter that He had long hair and didn't put it in a ponytail. It didn't matter who was with Him or who wasn't, and it certainly didn't matter if He carried something with Him or if He came empty-handed. I always looked forward to His visits. And the look on His face! The look that reminds me of so many times when He said to me, "I know things are hard, but remember what we've been through together." With those sparkling eyes He says, "I'm not going anywhere."

In the midst of the silence, in the midst of the questions, in the midst of the desire to know so much, I truly understand little. I think one of the hardest things in life is to realize that you really don't know very much. Comprehending the fact that you don't understand much of what you have seen in this life can send you in different directions. For me, being young and facing my own mortality shaped my life. It is a different experience when you're older. I don't know that it's something that can truly be explained. When you grow up talking about your own death, the death of others, and what it's like after a person dies, you have the opportunity to focus your thoughts and your heart upon what the purpose of life is all about.

Just because I was focused on the purpose of my life from a very young age doesn't mean that my thoughts and dreams have not wavered. It does mean that there was a place for God at all times, even during the times of great trial and tribulation.

So go ahead, ask, "Why?" But realize that you may never have a clear answer. It's all about God and living a life to His glory. This doesn't mean you always have things ironed out, but it does mean that you leave room for God to work in and through you. So as God does what He does best, do what you were created to do: hold His hand and take one step at a time. Praise God while you dance the road of life together. It may very well be the most difficult dance you have ever danced, but it is guaranteed to be the most beautiful dance you will ever remember. Be careful, because others are watching you. Others need to learn to dance with God too, and you never know if you will be the one to bring their hands together with God's. So dance, smile, and let God's light twinkle in your eyes and shine through your life.

Medical Miracle or God's Miracle?

> *"Lord, I'm thankful and amazed, in your image we are made—we have reason to celebrate."*
>
> Siler & Trevisick

There have been many times in my life that God has made His presence known in a quiet way. There have also been times when He spoke so loudly that those who didn't believe had to take a second look and question what they truly thought they believed. God has given us many reasons to celebrate, even in the midst of our difficulties. Yet so often we take the gifts God has provided only to return them gently or shove them back.

> *"Ask and it will be given to you; seek and you will find; knock and the door will be opened to you. For everyone who asks receives; the one who seeks finds; and to the one who knocks, the door will be opened."*
> *(Matthew 7:7-8, NIV)*

Why can't we take the words of scripture at face value when we are told to ask and it will be given to us? Why don't we take God seriously and just ask? Instead we mumble on and on, complaining about the situations we find ourselves in. God says:

- ask for what you need—for you will receive

- seek and look for that which calls out to your heart and you will find it
- for every door that comes across your path, knock - it will be opened

These are great and intense portions of God's Word that remind us of His presence, but also call us to action and belief. What are the desires of your heart? What are the needs of your soul? What do the doors you need to open look like?

The word 'miracle' can stir up differing thoughts and feelings in the lives of many people. Miracles are seen throughout the ministry of Jesus. He also calls His disciples to follow Him, teach, heal, and join Him in being the miracle in this world. Jesus gives us hope, direction, courage, and salvation. These are our reasons to celebrate!

When we ask God to enter our lives and we receive Him, that is a miracle. When we seek the presence of God and we find it, that is a miracle. When we knock and open our hearts, minds, and lives to what God has in store for us on the other side of the door, that is indeed a miracle.

A very important part of who I am, and an intricate part of my faith story, stems from the miracles of Jesus and how they have played out in my life. I have come to claim that one of the purposes of my life and ministry is to share the miracles God has done and not dwell on the one's that never took place from my limited perspective.

Growing up with so many physical ailments meant that I went to the doctor often. I don't remember dreading the doctor as many kids or even adults do. I attribute this to the fact that I was in the presence of medical staff so often that doctors' offices and hospitals truly became like home to me. That does not mean that I enjoyed the blood draws, catheters, surgeries, side effects of medications, missing birthday parties, being away from my brother, and spending my own birthday in the hospital. What it means is that this became a part of my life and my parents taught me to deal with it maturely. More importantly, I learned at an extremely young age that I was never alone. So, when my parents had to head home to take care of my brother or other day-to-day things, when I would lie in an isolation room, when I waited in the long sterile hallway counting dots on the acoustic ceiling tiles knowing my next stop was the operating room, when I was vigorously throwing up after surgery from the side effects of anesthesia, and when I tried desperately not to look at the clock on the wall across from my bed as the pain seemed more than I could bare - even then I was not alone. The God of the universe loved and cared for me, Kristine, in the midst of life.

Each of the trials I found myself in revealed a strong presence of God in one way or another. Some are certainly more vivid than others but each taught something to me or someone else, and often both. I learned a long time ago that my trials may have been for the purpose of allowing someone else to learn a lesson or see the presence of God for the first time by observing how I reacted or what I said. It never meant that I was excluded from some sort of gift from God, but many times it meant that the greatest gift was given to someone else. This story certainly gave me a great gift and an answer to prayer, but I believe it gave the medical staff an even greater sense of humbly receiving a gift at the same time.

In scripture Jesus is referred to as the "great physician." I relate to this description and the many intricacies it provides in my life and the lives of others. Jesus as the great physician reminds me that He is concerned not just for my physical health but my emotional, psychological, mental, and spiritual health. Anything that needs repair God can put back together. God does not always put us back together like Humpty Dumpty. Often we are put back together in a new and better way. If we break a bone it can either be mended or made better and stronger than it was before. God puts things in the place they need to be and if that means right back where they were then that is where they end up. If they need to be stronger and filled with a glorious story of God's power then that is how things end up.

In my experience, the latter is how most situations end. God finds ways to utilize the difficult places we find ourselves in and provides an opportunity for His Glory to rise above it all. When this takes place, we are not just asked but are mandated by God to share these experiences that show God's glory to others. The key to the miracles in my life is that they continue to be the story of Jesus.

As people struggle with their faith they often need proof that God can actually do things of great power. I guess that is how I have looked at my life. I have many stories with strong proof that even stumps and shocks the best of physicians. When you are a physician and are up against God, the greatest physician of all time, you are bound to learn something if you are willing to admit you don't have all the answers. If you are wise you not only learn but are humbled as well.

Do you believe in miracles? I don't mean the ones you read about in the Bible, although that is a good place to start. I am asking about today's miracles, miracles that stop you in your tracks and cause you to become speechless and in awe of what you have witnessed. I must say without hesitation, yes! Yes, I believe in miracles! I believe that miracles take place in order to allow the power and glory of God to shine so that we stay focused on where the power originates. Ultimately, just because I have been the recipient of many miracles, the miracle is not about me, but instead it is all about God! It is about the power and glory that God chose to shine in my life.

Every person knows what it is like to be sick: to wake up with a cold right before a big presentation, or to come down with the flu as you head to a huge family celebration. Some have dealt with chronic or acute pain or a life threatening illness. You can name your own illness. Of course your illness may not be physical in the sense I am speaking of. Perhaps it is the end of a long relationship, the death of a loved one, or an addiction that has placed you in a difficult spot in life. Regardless, pain is present. Pain is the focus and pain is what stops us from doing what we need, want, or hope to do. For me, once again it was a physical pain in my leg, and this one scared me tremendously.

The fall of 2003 I found that when I would stand in the same position for longer than ten minutes my right leg would go numb. When I would try and walk I wasn't sure where my leg was, where it would land and, most importantly, I wasn't sure it would hold me up. Have I mentioned I hate falling? This condition continued for quite some time and progressively got worse. I only told a few people of the situation because I didn't want to scare anyone. At this time I was working as a parish pastor who specialized in youth and family ministry. When anyone works with youth you are always on the move! There is no time to stop and be ill or even slow down.

Over time the symptoms got worse, and by Easter the next spring I had little movement or feeling in my right leg. I had lost most of the muscle tone in both of my legs and even with strong medication the pain was almost more than I could bear. The only thing that had been determined by this time was that my leg wasn't the problem, it was my back. I felt lost, alone, and questioned what the future held for me. The first surgeon I saw felt that with my intricate history and present situation it was too complicated for him to proceed, so he referred me to another surgeon. While I appreciated his honesty that this was beyond his skill and knowledge, I felt more lost and alone. I felt like I was starting over - yet again!

Throughout this time, prayers were being lifted on my behalf, even though no one knew what they were really praying for. Three and a half weeks later I met with a world-renowned surgeon. I held great hope that he would know what to do; after all, he was world-renowned. More tests were ordered. Some of these tests were new to me which raised my anxiety quite a bit. After the results were in, my husband and I met with the surgeon in hopes that we would know what our next step would be. All along, we had been told that this was a disk issue. These new tests revealed something no one expected. The situation was much more complicated than anyone had thought, including the surgeon. It was discovered that two tumors were embedded at the base of my spinal cord which was also tethered. This was not an easy surgery and the potential complications were not easy to swallow. The part that made it even more difficult was that the surgeon would not do the surgery due to the potential risks. A tethered cord is usually a pediatric complexity and is much riskier when present in an adult. Through conversations with my family and many hours of prayer and even more tears, I knew that the surgery needed to be done. I was only getting worse - by this time I could barely walk.

I knew full well that the surgery might not work. I understood I might wake up paralyzed and incontinent, but I also knew that if I didn't try I would be in a wheelchair for the rest of my life anyway. I also knew that God would be with me even though I felt terribly afraid. I always thought with each surgery the fear would decrease, but I have found that sometimes it is harder because I know so much about the process. After several conversations with the surgeon, he hesitantly agreed to take on this difficult surgery.

Surgery was scheduled for June 4th - my dad's birthday. I was blessed to have my husband, my parents, my brother, sister-in-law, and my niece there for support. I must say having my niece there, nine months old at the time, was such a gift. Children always have a way of making me laugh even in the midst of crisis. This was her job along with the never-ending hugs and kisses. (Thanks Hailey!)

Three days prior to surgery I had the most vivid recollection of the Biblical story in Mark 2 where the onlookers in the crowd listened to Jesus. These people were desperate to get close enough that they could see Jesus. There was a man who was ill, a paralytic. Because of the crowd his friends couldn't get him to Jesus. These were great friends and were his deep support system. They knew their friend only needed to hear the word of Jesus and he would be made well. The crowd was so large they couldn't plow through the doors to push the people aside. So, they decided to raise him up, take the roof off the building and lower him in to see Jesus. Jesus commented on their faith, and I like to think, of their creative way to get in to see Him. A debate took place there that day regarding the difficulty of forgiving sins or healing the man. Jesus spoke the words to heal the man to show that He had the power to heal by forgiving sins and to heal him physically.

I knew at that moment that all I needed was to touch Jesus, to hear the word of Jesus, and I'd be healed, but there was no way I could get there on my own. It was then that I realized the prayers being offered on my behalf by literally thousands of people across the country are what brought me in through the roof so that Jesus could touch me, say the words and heal me. The miracle of this surgery was so powerful that when I allow myself to return in thought and spirit I am still overwhelmed by the grace, mercy, and healing power of God. You see, the world-renowned surgeon who was hesitant to perform this surgery, as well as the first surgeon who stated this was too complex for him, were both pleasantly surprised and humbled by the results. What had been indicated on the MRI's, CT scans and x-rays were not what was found when they opened me up. My spinal cord was not tethered. There were not two tumors, but one. They looked very hard to find the second one, but it just wasn't there. To top things off, the tumor they did find was not embedded in my spinal cord but was between the vertebrae, self-contained around the nerves. During my surgery, a third surgeon was called in to remove this simple cyst, because the world renowned surgeon was not as well versed in less complex situations. I vividly remember waking up after surgery as my husband, mother, and father entered the elevator with me to take me to my room. I immediately realized the surgery was over and I could move my feet. I knew I would walk even though I had no idea of the miracle that had just taken place.

The day I was being discharged from the hospital, the world-renowned surgeon came to visit. You could see in his face the sense of relief he was filled with. He had carried much stress prior to my surgery because it was likely that the surgery would not be a success. He spoke to me and my family about how puzzled and confused he was by the turn of events. My family and I just smiled and told him it brought clarity, not confusion, to us. We told him we knew who carried the true burden that encompassed this circumstance. It provided an explanation that once again God's healing power and presence is in the here and now. We do not know to what extent he took our explanation, but we could see the wheels turning in his mind as he left my room.

The miracle that took place that day - the miracle that carried me to the feet of Jesus because I couldn't get there on my own - overwhelms me to this day. This is a message that proclaims the miraculous power of Christ, that He is alive and continues to work in our lives. Christ's presence does indeed give us hope, direction, courage, salvation, and most certainly a reason to celebrate! So pause, feel God's presence in your life and allow yourself to celebrate that miracle, as well as those that are to come!

Full Circle

There are days when it seems just about impossible to believe that I have only had a firm diagnosis for a little over a decade. Throughout my life there were numerous different diagnoses, many of which were wrong. Those who diagnosed me correctly often arrived at their conclusion based on one, maybe two characteristics, meaning they were able to diagnose a specific problem but never the underlying issue. Imagine living your entire childhood and many years of adulthood knowing you had a complicated illness, but no one knew what it was or how to treat it. In reality, the surgeries I have had throughout my life were done as things came up or got worse. There was no direction and no anticipation of what might be right around the corner. As the circle began to connect itself, I remembered: God already knew everything, and in time He would supply the necessary answers.

When I was young, there was certainly a better sense of what might need to be done, because most of the complexities of my illness were present at birth in one form or another, even if the doctors didn't know what was wrong. For example, it was obvious that I had a lot of tumors, some visible to the naked eye, while others were seen only on images intricate machinery could provide. Regardless of how we learned about them, it became clear that they would be detrimental to my growth, movement, and freedom from pain. Needless to say, it seemed that with every new doctor I saw, someone thought they had **THE** diagnosis. It was difficult to go to the doctor and have a simple cold. Something bigger and more critical always crept into the conversation. Many times doctors wanted their day in the spotlight to say they had discovered something grand and unique.

The summer of 2001 I was eager to preach over the weekend and send a group of school-aged children off to camp. I would join them later in the week. Friday night arrived and I felt a little worn out, but it was a Friday after a long week. My husband Bill and I had a very busy Saturday and still I felt pretty weak and tired. Sunday I preached at all three services, and by the time the morning was over I didn't feel much like going to a fundraising basketball tournament I was expected to attend. Much to my and others' disappointment, I went home and climbed into bed, feeling more exhausted than I had in a long time. Monday morning rolled around and I ventured off to work, where a short time later I had difficulty speaking to our church secretary without getting out of breath. I had a doctor's appointment that afternoon, and to my great disappointment, I needed to call Bill and ask him to meet me at the hospital I was being admitted to.

Due to my many allergies, an accurate diagnosis can be difficult. I am not only allergic to numerous common medications but also several medications which are used to help diagnose. Later that night, we learned that I had a pulmonary embolism, a blood clot blocking the main artery of my left lung. No wonder it had become difficult to breathe! Some might jokingly say this was when I was the quietest in my life. After a day or two of good rest and staying in bed, I felt quite well. Yet, I was not permitted to get out of bed for fear that the clot would move and cause a more critical situation. So I lied in bed for over a week and didn't join the kids at camp. It broke my heart to call and tell them I wouldn't be there. My heart began to mend when they stopped by the hospital on their way home to wish me well with a bucket hat covered with words of encouragement and their signatures. This hospitalization began my experience of taking Coumadin, a blood thinner. Oddly enough, numerous members of my church took Coumadin, and most of them wanted to talk about how many milligrams they took each day and what their INR numbers were each week (a number which lets you know how thin or thick your blood is). Because I was younger and it wasn't known exactly why I had the blood clot in the first place, I had to take additional precautions. The thinness of my blood was increased to a higher level than normal, meaning that I took a higher dosage of the medication. This made for fun conversations with fellow Coumadin consumers who were taking significantly less than I was. Six months later I was taken off the Coumadin. I was so thankful that I had no further blood clots and no complications while I was on the blood thinner.

Life continued with few interruptions until one afternoon a few months later. I had been visiting numerous members of our church in several different hospitals. By the third hospital I began to wonder if I was imagining how I felt. I continued on and travelled to the last two hospitals, much closer to our home. While at the last hospital it became very difficult to breathe. When I think back on it now, I think of how stupid I was. God had nudged me and I refused to listen. In each hospital I visited I thought of stopping at the emergency department, but convinced myself that I had everything under control. So I finished visiting a few more patients, got in my car and went back to work. Of course when the rest of the staff saw me they put me in their car and drove me to the emergency room of the hospital I had just visited. Fortunately I was greeted by one of our church members who was a nurse in the emergency room. I wasn't visiting this time; I was admitted, yet again. Unfortunately, things were worse than last time. Now there were three embolisms found - two in one lung and one in the other. I quickly realized how critical this was. I had been so fortunate the year before but didn't realize until this happened how great the risk to my life had been. We learned it was even riskier because, once again, there was no known source of the clot. All we knew was the clots ended up in my lungs; we didn't know where they came from, like in most people. So, once again, I perplexed the doctors.

This time, I was put back on Coumadin, at a higher dosage with no chance of ever coming off of it. In addition, I didn't recover very well this time. I struggled with my breathing, energy, and strength for months. My doctors had no idea what to do. So they sent me to the Mayo Clinic in Rochester, MN.

The Mayo Clinic Hospital was only a few hours drive from our home. In fact, Bill and I had been there to visit members of our church before and, because of the conference space available, we had been there to attend conferences in the past. This time though, I was the patient. This time there was no fun involved, and no smiles. We spent an entire week there so I could have tests done and meet numerous, different types of doctors. The only piece of information we walked away with was that my breathing had been compromised and there was nothing that could be done to make it easier and less painful to breathe. The pulmonary embolisms had done damage. I felt as if I already knew that before spending the week there. I was told that this was my new baseline - my new normal.

One of the recommendations was that I meet with a geneticist for more extensive testing to determine my genetic make-up. They were pretty sure they could find many additional things wrong with me, but did not feel confident about an overall diagnosis. After much thought and prayer I decided not to proceed. I then threw myself into Scripture. I had traveled to all of those appointments with great apprehension. During one of the tests, alone on a hard, cold table trying not to cry, God answered my prayer and provided direction for my future. I realized I was done. I had searched my entire life for a diagnosis. I had been through more tests, blood draws, contraptions, and relived my history more times than I cared to remember. It really didn't matter to me what I had. I didn't need an official diagnosis. I had lived more than 30 years without one, so why did I need one now? Even though it was suggested strongly that I proceed, I clung to the words *"a time to search and a time to give up" (Ecclesiastes 3:6, NIV).* After 30+ years, it was okay to stop searching.

Not only did I feel support, but I felt freedom. I had freedom that, diagnosis or not, I was still me. Diagnosis or not, I still had my story and my future. Diagnosis or not, there was still hope in Christ. I must admit I wasn't really sure what the hope was for, but I knew it promised me more freedom than struggling through more intensive tests to risk knowing nothing more than I'd known to date. If a diagnosis was made there would also be the fear and anticipation of other complications yet to follow. I did not want to live in fear like that. The book of Ecclesiastes reminded me that there is a time for everything and for everything there is a purpose. I certainly didn't know what the purpose was for this trip to all of these new doctors and new tests which discovered nothing new, but what I did know was that God had a purpose behind it. Perhaps one day I would learn this purpose, perhaps not.

So I returned to see my primary physician so she could receive an update on the intensive trip. Unfortunately, she was extremely discouraged by what she heard. Since very little clarity was brought to the table from the best of the best, she didn't feel it was in my best interest to treat me anymore. Her knowledge was limited and it was obvious that there were critical things going on with me. I was then referred to another doctor for my general care. I was sad for this news because I really liked this doctor, and I can be pretty tough on physicians. I expect a lot and need very clear communication. Not all doctors are capable of providing clear communication and integrating the patient in their own care. She did this, and she trusted me. It would be difficult to move on, and in the middle of a medical crisis too. She referred me to an internal medicine physician. He wanted to begin with a few standard tests to get his own baseline of what was going on. Most of these tests came back fine, as expected. I received a call one day requesting I come in to speak with him. This wise and gentle man entered the room, with a heavy heart. He had news; good and bad. The good news was that he discovered what had been giving me the intense pain and causing more difficulty with my breathing. The bad news was that it wasn't going to be an easy fix, if there was one at all. I had herniated disks in my neck near the vertebrae which were already beginning to fuse themselves. In other words, my neck was cementing itself in a very bad position, permanently. This meant more new doctors, most likely surgery resulting in little movement in my neck for the rest of my life. I left the doctor's appointment in tears and drove home.

The new adventure had begun: to find a physician who would accept me as a patient, suggest options for treatment, and then be willing to follow through and actually treat me. This was very difficult due to my bone structure and recent history of multiple pulmonary embolisms. The embolisms frightened most of them, especially since they were recent, multiple, and had no known source. This was not a good combination.

While we were dealing with how to proceed, it is important to remember that the rest of what makes up my disease doesn't usually sit on the sidelines and watch. More often than not, when one thing needs attention, something else creeps to center stage seeking the spotlight. So, in reality, there is always something going on and many times there are several things going on at once. This time was no different.

When I was very young I had part of a lymphangioma - a lymphatic tumor - removed from under my right arm. To this day I can still feel a part of the tumor, and when it becomes aggravated by bumping my arm, having blood pressure taken, or blood draws with a tourniquet, the tumor can go into anger mode and remain inflamed for months. Throughout my life we learned little tricks and implemented them into my treatment. No more tourniquets above the elbow and no more blood pressures on my right arm. Unfortunately, these alone don't keep the tumor from becoming aggravated. Sometimes for no reason it would inflame and become very painful. In addition, now some of the tumor was seeping out through the decades - old incision. Pretty gross, huh? Regardless of what it looked like, it was painful and, with it being under my arm, rubbed against itself and clothing, causing more irritation. As the circle continued to connect itself, God's hidden plan directed me to a dermatologist at the University of Minnesota.

Venturing off to yet another physician proved to be part of God's plan all along. Not only was I able to be treated, but we had the greatest discovery to date. Keep in mind that this new physician had a specific job: to treat the lymphangioma under my arm. As with most physicians, when they meet a new patient there is always a time of getting connected and learning the medical history of the patient. For a fairly minor issue, this physician had a lot of history to gather. During his intake of my medical history, Bill and I recounted the recent story of my pulmonary embolisms and difficulty that came with them. In addition, we shared that I did not have an overall diagnosis. My interactions with this physician were few. First we met for consultation and suggested treatment. The second visit he surgically removed the lymphangioma under my arm in his office. Lastly, I went for a post-surgical follow up visit to make sure everything had healed well and to make sure I had all of my questions answered. During this last appointment, the physician made a suggestion. Being at a University, it was a teaching hospital. In the teaching, "Grand Rounds" took place where different patients came to be seen by numerous physicians for potential suggestions of treatment, for students to learn and, sometimes, for a diagnosis. My physician informed me that the next set of Grand Rounds would be headed by a world-renowned geneticist who had been made aware of my case. It was strongly suggested that I agree to attend.

A couple of weeks later I attended the Grand Rounds. I sat in a hospital gown with my bare feet dangling over the edge of the cold table, in an even colder room. As I waited, I wondered if my life would be any different afterward. One by one, groups of eight to twelve physicians entered my room at a time. With each visit I was asked numerous questions as they looked over most of my body. Included in one of the groups was the world-renowned geneticist. It was disappointing to me that he only asked one question and was in the room for less than 90 seconds. I wanted to run, and fast. What a waste of my time - AGAIN!

After the last group of physicians exited my room, I was told I could get dressed and leave. I went home, very sad that I had been led down another dead end road. I questioned why God had me travel back down this path when there was no answer. I also felt deprived of the time I thought I would have with the geneticist and felt it was only for the young students to see medical anomalies they might not see elsewhere. In many ways, I felt used.

A little over a week later, the physician who directed me to the Grand Rounds called. He wanted me to know that the geneticist was fairly certain he knew what disease I had. I silently wondered how in such a short time with me he could know much of anything about me. It was called Proteus-like Syndrome. He called it "Proteus-like" because it was not quite the same as Proteus Syndrome. In Proteus the describing characteristics are <u>not</u> present at birth, as mine were. This was the only differentiation. Proteus Syndrome causes an overgrowth of skin, bones, muscles, fatty tissues, and blood and lymphatic vessels.

I quickly turned to the internet, although in 2002 there was not nearly the information there is today. I read the characteristics and medical complications and realized it almost perfectly described me. There were actually other people in the world that were like me. One important thing to know about Proteus is that no two people have the same combination of symptoms or to the same degree. I am extremely fortunate that my brain was not affected by my disease, as most Proteus patients experience. There is a very limited number of people diagnosed with Proteus; approximately 120 worldwide. Most do not live into their 20's. Blood clots and pulmonary embolisms are the most common cause of death. The pulmonary embolisms I had recently dealt with were a transition to more unexpected and serious traits of my disease. Even though there was still no site of origin for my blood clots, I was very thankful to be on a higher than normal dose of Coumadin.

The Grand Rounds was not an accident. In addition, it was not an accident that I needed to have this lymphangioma treated while dealing with the recovery from three pulmonary embolisms or herniated disks in my neck. It was all a part of a bigger picture, God's greater plan to complete the circle. Remember the herniated disks in my neck? The surgeons who turned me away because I was considered high risk for surgery? By the time it was discovered that I had Proteus-like Syndrome, my neck pain had subsided to a tolerable level, and to this day no further intervention has been needed. So far the disks have fused to a manageable position. When I think back, I wonder if I had not gone to have the lymphangioma under my arm treated, would I have jumped into surgery because the pain was too intense and I desperately wanted relief? I will never know, but I believe that God would have found another way to lead me down my path had I acted in haste.

Over the course of the next several years, the pain from my vascular system increased. My venous and lymphatic systems are like a large bowl of spaghetti, and when they get inflamed, the pain is much worse. By the time I decided I needed to look into my options, it was not only difficult to move but it was painful to wear clothing. Once again we went down the road to find a physician who not only would see me, but also treat me. Once again there was great fear for my pulmonary embolisms and the greater risks that come with them. We were fortunately connected with a physician who met with me and requested I have series of new tests. There are some days when I think I have had every test created in medicine. I know this is not true, but I am occasionally certain I am close to getting there.

Bill and I met with the physician after the results were in. Sadly, he felt I was too complex for his ability. Instead he referred me to a physician who had perfected a new procedure to treat vascular malformations. This physician was in Denver, Colorado and at this point in our lives, we lived near Phoenix, Arizona.

We began this new process by having phone conversations and sending my records, including the results of my most recent tests. Another hurdle arose, as my insurance company was not willing to pay for this treatment the physician offered, even if I was a candidate for it. Their reasoning was that it was a new procedure and the physician was out of state. That was only the beginning of the insurance complications.

The physician in Colorado had taken a look at my history and recent test results. He let me know that he wanted to meet me in person and have additional tests to map my vascular system in order to determine if I was indeed a candidate for this procedure. A short time later, after numerous pleas, letters and research, the insurance company provided the authorization for me to proceed. We were on our way to Colorado.

Bill and I went with hopes that I would be a candidate for this new approach and treatment, even though we did not know much about it yet. If approved, I would have my first procedure the day after my next set of tests. We were able to stay at a beautiful hotel that offered patients a wonderfully discounted "hospital rate."

We first met with the physician, had the tests and met with him again that same afternoon. He determined some very important things. First, my vascular malformations did not affect my arteries, only my veins. This was great news as it made things a lot less challenging and complicated. I rarely heard those words related to me and my medical needs before, so at first I was not sure I heard him right. He went on to explain that I was most certainly a candidate for this procedure. We were on for first thing the next morning.

Bill and I learned that I would be put under general anesthesia for the procedure. I would have an arteriogram at the onset to aid in knowing exactly where they wanted to treat this time around. The procedure consisted of injecting the ends of the malformed veins with nearly pure ethanol. Yes, you read that right: ethanol, like what goes in your car. The whole idea kind of freaked me out at first: ethanol in my veins? Basically what takes place is the ethanol singes the ends of the malformed veins and they die off. It is important for you to know that these are not veins that have the purpose of supplying blood to different parts of my body, but instead are extra veins that get inflamed, irritated, and are in the way of normal function.

Along with allergies to different medications, I have always had horrific reactions to general anesthesia. I wake up from surgery with fluid in my ears causing intense nausea and vomiting combined with vertigo that can last weeks after surgery. My fear was experiencing this side effect and then boarding a plane to go home the next day. I had never had to travel to this extent for surgery before. I was delighted to learn that this physician had a "medicinal cocktail" they used for extreme nausea and vomiting, post anesthesia. I was game to try it out as the reaction couldn't be much worse than what I already anticipated. I was given special medications before, during, and after surgery, and in the days that followed. I was truly blessed that this combination of medications worked extremely well for me, as I was eating shortly after I woke up. I not only was gifted with a treatment to the painful vascular system, but learned a new way to deal with my post-anesthesia complications.

Unfortunately, I had one unexpected complication after returning home. It was discovered after much research that the ethanol caused drug-induced Lupus in my system. I did not have Lupus, but my body reacted to the ethanol as if I did, so the pain and discomfort associated with a Lupus flare took weeks of medication and rest to subside. In the next five months I had three additional treatments. With each additional treatment the dose of ethanol was increased as my body did not react to it adversely, outside of the Lupus pain. The last two treatments were done two days in a row with a much higher dose of ethanol injected, allowing the physician to ablate many more veins. Oddly enough, I woke up the morning after the first treatment with a red nose, like someone who drinks too much alcohol might have. I thought it would have been fair if I had been able to enjoy the effects of ethanol in a different way.

After my third treatment, my insurance company informed me that I would soon cap my insurance coverage if I continued to receive the treatments. Fortunately, the pain had subsided greatly. In addition my physician felt strongly that these vascular malformations were likely the culprit of my spontaneous pulmonary embolisms. This certainly explained why I did not have clots in my legs or arms - with most of my malformations being in the trunk area, they aligned with my lungs.

I continue to be amazed at God's timing and how I am guided to and from different aspects of life. God truly has a plan that intricately connects all aspects of my life. After working as a parish pastor for over ten years, I found myself in transition related to my vocation. In a short time, God provided the opportunity for me to move into hospital chaplaincy. I far exceeded the requirements of my denomination and knew in my heart that I had a gift for this type of ministry, because I easily understood the complexities of being a patient. The door opened, ironically, by my accepting a position at the Mayo Clinic in Arizona. I had considered hospital chaplaincy at numerous times in my life, but never dreamed I would work for this top institution. This decision was purely God nudging me in the direction I was meant to go.

A year or so after I started this ministry, I began to have similar problems with the vascular malformations I'd had before. They were irritated and causing pain. It was discovered by one of my other physicians that ethanol ablations were now done at Mayo. I made arrangements to have another treatment done, close to home, and under local anesthesia. The physician who treated me had been recently trained by the doctor in Colorado. Things sure improved for me! After this single treatment, I learned that there were not nearly as many veins as earlier projected needing treatment. This was amazing news, because initially we anticipated a minimum of 25 treatments just to get things under control.

Life has come full circle for me, many times over. The long story of no accurate diagnosis, unresolved pulmonary embolisms, multiple medical issues creating room for one another, cutting edge medical treatments, new medicinal cocktails, and a new job all provided fresh arenas for God's plan to be brought to fruition. With each stage I could see and feel the hand of God. I never dreamed that a severe complication of my disease could end up being treated not long after I was diagnosed and leading me down a new career path.

Life is full of many puzzle pieces that often do not feel as if they fit together. Ultimately all of the disjointed-feeling steps of my life completed a circle I began walking years ago. When I feel as if I am at an end or am stuck, I may only be at the beginning of another round of adventures. In time, God will reveal the road before each one of us as our hearts are refined by His goodness. The story is never done because it begins and ends with the infinite God.

Unexpected Gifts

Most people find themselves thinking about their future at some point, perhaps even several times, as life reveals new dreams, desires, successes, and failures. As we continue to develop our morals, beliefs, and values, we continue to process and renew who we truly want to be. The older we become, the less time we have to adjust our life's direction and plan. All the while God continues to have His plan for our lives.

Children dream of what they want to be when they grow up. Most of the time this decision or dream changes several times before choosing a career path. Regardless of whether we are dreaming of a vocation, where we may live, or how to spend our spare time, there are many things we plan for and dream of. Do I get married or have children? What are my hobbies? Am I involved in my community? What do I truly care about? These may be only a few of the questions we consider as we grow older, but the bottom line is: how do we envision our lives?

As a child I imagined myself married with five children, twin girls and triplet boys. I would work as one of three things: a parish pastor, a school teacher, or a hospital chaplain. I never really thought about where I would live, probably because I thought I would always live in California. There would be a part of me that still loved to be in the outdoors making s'mores and fishing at a nearby creek. I would still have a daring side to me that loved jeep rides, roller-coasters, and trips to nowhere specific. On the other hand, I would love making things for others and would be a great cook, greeting neighbors with baskets of goodies to welcome them to the neighborhood. One thing that was a part of my future vision, known by only a few people, is that I didn't see my life past 27 years of age. I had no reason to think this. Perhaps it was some internal fear of planning too much, or not wanting to look beyond where I was unable to envision myself. I don't know. Needless to say, as I approached the ripe old age of 25, I began to get a bit fearful of each birthday. Since I am writing this nearly two decades later, I didn't die at (or prior to) my 27th birthday. But once I hit 28 I began reflecting on my life and adjusting parts of it that needed a new vision.

Today's reality includes the fact that I am married. I have two grown step-children who lived with their mother their entire childhood. I have no biological children. I have many children of various ages for whom I am their "second mother" due to the depth and nature of the relationship. As I reflect upon my desire for several children, I know now that God was the One who truly knew better. My body could never have handled bearing children, and I would have probably spent much of my pregnancies confined to bed. (I am not one who enjoys being bedridden and having others do everything for me.) Once the children were born I would never have had the physical strength needed to take care of them. God's answer of "no" to one of the deepest desires of my heart can still bring me to tears. I now understand why God made the decision He did, but sometimes it is still hard to accept. I know that God made this decision out of love for me.

Honestly, my strength and energy continue to decline as I age. As a mother I would not have served my children well, and God knew that. These are the times when I realize that God always knows best. God knows what choices and decisions of today will affect our lives and the lives of others before they are even made. Not having children is still the greatest disappointment of my life, and even though it is painful, I thank God for children and even not allowing me to have my own.

I earned a bachelor's degree in Speech Communication, with minors in Music and Psychology. The year after graduating from college I worked full time as a Youth and Education Director. Approximately half way through that year I made a decision regarding my vocational direction. I went on to receive a Master's in Divinity four years later. I became a parish pastor for ten years, working mostly in youth and family ministry. I have worked as a hospital chaplain the past several years. I did live in California until a few years after I was married, at which time parish ministry took us to Iowa, Minnesota, Arizona, and Nebraska. I got a flavor of living in different parts of the country, each with their own unique characteristics. I do enjoy making s'mores and fishing, as long as I can sit down. My most recent fishing expeditions with my husband have proved that I am a better fisherman in a small creek where I am less likely to break fishing rods or tangle my line. For example, the first time my husband took me fishing I broke three fishing rods the first half of the morning. Needless to say I read and napped the rest of the day, something I am much better at. Okay, so I can't fish ... but God did say we are to fish for people and not just for food, right?

Speaking of food, I can cook. When I really need to step in and be responsible for our family meals, we survive. In fact neither of us has become sick from my cooking yet. But I married a man who is a phenomenal cook! My husband learned out of the need for survival at a young age how to cook. Somewhere in there, it became more than survival but a love for cooking and gifting others with incredible food. He is a creative cook, who just throws a bit of this and that in something and it always turns out wonderful. Those who are fortunate enough to be present hide their drooling in an effort to be invited back for more wonderful food. There are foods that I swore I would never eat, and now they are among my favorites. As his wife I encourage this gift whenever possible. I am definitely not the cook I thought I would be. Another gift from God: at the end of the day when I need my rest the most, my sweet husband is in the kitchen fixing something nutritious and yummy to feed my body and soul. No need to be on my feet. I am pampered and just sit and wait for dinner to be served. God gave me a husband who not only cooks but cleans (he is pickier about how clean the bathroom is than I am!) and does the laundry too. I am no ordinary housewife because the gift of my husband has spared energy for me to do other things that I am better at and enjoy. What a gift!

The other part of my life's vision was that I knew my body would decline at a different rate than others. This was not too difficult until my mid-thirties. At that time I had to admit my body was not as strong as it had been. Being in my thirties and finding my body declining was not a part of my plan. I expected it earlier than others but I thought that meant more like in my sixties. I was finding it very difficult to travel, and going to amusement parks became more like painful work than fun. After lots of conversations with others, prayer, and self-talk I got a wheelchair for only those things. When I would fly out of and to a large airport I would use my wheelchair. If I went to an amusement park like Disneyland, out came the wheelchair. I found that I enjoyed myself more but continued to struggle with the reality that I couldn't do everything on my own. If it was just family I did much better, but when friends and people I didn't know very well saw me in the wheelchair, or even needed to push me, I felt a part of myself becoming ashamed and angry. This was not who I expected myself to be, and even more so, I was not able to do the things I wanted to do by myself. I had to realize I needed help. I also had to accept it.

The physical difficulties of my life had always been met with an "I'll do it if it kills me" attitude. I would try and try until I succeeded. Since the age of two, when I figured out how to release the soft restraints which were to restrict my movement to lying in bed after major foot surgery there has been no stopping me. The purpose of the restraints was to keep me from standing on my foot, injuring myself, or compromising the effects of the surgery. I must have thought this was nonsense because as soon as I stood up I was a happy camper. I also remember the zeal of wheelchair races with other kids down the halls of the hospital, until the janitor had a look of fury when I ran into the sand-filled ashtray in front of the elevators. What was he going to do, tell a five year old girl in a wheelchair to clean it up?

Children have a way of working through things that adults seem to lose. That is why I believe Jesus tells us to come to Him like a child. When we are children we trust, believe, and hope. As we grow we lose many of those instincts that allow us to go on. I too have lost that part of myself on several occasions. I thought getting a wheelchair for extended events was hard. Six years later I was faced with another challenge that tore me apart.

Life was good physically for several years. After my daily pain got under control I felt like myself again, meeting challenges head on with energy and excitement. I loved my job as a chaplain and worked several weekend 24-48 hour shifts and weekly 5:00pm-8:00am shifts in addition to my regular daily job. I felt so good, and even on the weekends and nights I didn't work I was ready for anything. I enjoyed family, friends, and hobbies. Life was good!

My husband and I often ran our weekly errands on Fridays because when we worked in the parish that was usually our day off. One Friday afternoon we decided to go to all four grocery stores that we often shopped at so that Saturday could be a day without commitments, just the two of us. We had finished shopping at the first store and were stopped getting ready to enter traffic on our way to the next store when there was a CRASH! We were hit from behind while we were stopped. After the initial shock wore off, my husband asked how I was. My neck and low back hurt, which was kind of a "duh!" moment for me. He instructed me not to move as he got out and spoke to the other driver. The pain increased and he then had me call 911. There was no fear, no time to think. The EMT crew arrived and asked their standard questions. It was decided that I should go to the emergency room by ambulance. I had never been in an ambulance before. The fear level rose as I realized that this may have ruined more than just our afternoon. My husband drove our car so that he at least would have a ride home. I requested going to the hospital in which I worked, because I knew the staff and the quality of care. I had been a visitor to the hospital closest to where we lived, and I wouldn't send anyone there. Since my injuries were not deemed life threatening, we were on our way to where I worked. I called my boss and colleagues from the ambulance to let them know I was heading to the emergency room as a patient. It was a Friday late afternoon and we hit traffic. Despite this I knew the drive was worth it. I was also fortunate that even though the emergency room was very busy when we arrived, my favorite emergency room physician was directed to care for me. Thank you, God!

The bottom line was that my body had been strained very badly. To a normal person this would mean pain and discomfort for a few days or maybe a week. For me it was much worse. Let me take you back briefly … remember I have an 'I will do it if it kills me' attitude? Well, I went to work for the next two weeks. The staff I work with had not only visited me in the emergency room and prayed with us but they also took my night and weekend calls during those first weeks after the accident. Unfortunately I only began to feel worse. In working with my physician it was finally decided that I needed to go on Short Term Disability. I cried for weeks. I knew I couldn't take care of this on my own. My husband needed to help care for me. I had no energy, only pain. I endured over a year of physical therapy. I returned to work slowly after a few months, but I did not return to night duty.

About 16 months after the accident, I knew that I truly was not going to ever be the same. I couldn't stand for longer than a couple of minutes without needing to sit. My walking speed had become a snail's crawl and the excruciating pain and lack of controlled leg motion set in after approximately 40 feet. I had to rearrange my daily routine at work which wasn't the worst part. After walking to my car at the end of the day I was in tears from the pain. Then I had a 37 mile drive home in traffic. I could not see myself doing this much longer. Each time my physician or husband would bring up the conversation of my not getting better I began to shut down. I knew one day I would be at this point physically, but not this soon. Not now. I felt limited, did not enjoy life, and had lost a part of myself. What I did know was this was not who I was or what I stood for.

In May 2010, just prior to my 41st birthday, I purchased a scooter to use mostly at work or if we went on long excursions, like to the mall or a museum. Being in a wheelchair does allow relief but little independence unless you have the upper body strength to move it easily yourself, which I do not. It took me quite some time to be able to even say the words "I am getting a scooter" without crying. I felt defeated and as if I let myself down. But I also knew that if I wanted to have any sort of life and continue working at a job I loved, I had to do this. Putting all of that together was very difficult for me. The weeks leading up to having the scooter delivered and having a lift put on my vehicle so that I could actually go somewhere outside of my house seemed to take forever. I even considered canceling the order, thinking "I should be able to live without this." The day before my scooter was scheduled for delivery I saw a woman, approximately my age, in our hospital lobby sitting in her scooter. She was happy, laughing, smiling, and living her life. In fact, I noticed her before I noticed the scooter. Then I had a long chat with myself. The scooter was not Kris. Kris was not going to become the scooter. My personality and all I stood for was not going to change. What would change is that now I could move faster than I ever could have, my pain would be reduced, my energy would increase, and I would be more independent, allowing for excursions by myself.

So when the scooter arrived I wanted to use it right away. I had a couple of days off work and I went on a trip to the mall all by myself. I was gone for hours. I had not been to the mall in over a year. What a day that was! I didn't have to depend on anyone but myself. Even though this was good practice, my first day going to work with it was very difficult. I did great until I entered the building. Then all I could do was cry. A friend of mine met me that day before I left for home and reminded me that this was an adjustment time and soon I would be adjusted to this new way of life. While we were talking someone else I knew casually came up and asked the question I hate the most: "what happened?" I wanted to say, "I hardly know you - it's none of your business," but my friend spoke first and said I was entering new territory and nothing had happened. From that moment on I realized what I would say when people would ask what happened; I now respond, "I finally decided it was time to take care of myself."

In all reality this is true. It took me a long time to admit that I wasn't able to do everything for myself. Life is better with the scooter, but I do have to work very hard at things when I don't have it with me. I don't want to become completely dependent on my three wheels, so I must exercise my legs because they do not get as much exercise each day. I find the time when I am out without the scooter a bit scary, but fortunately I am often not alone. Now, years later, attempts are made to deck out my scooter for particular holidays and notice I am not the only one with wheels.

The unexpected gifts keep coming into my life. Sometimes they do not seem like gifts at first, but when I look closely at the whole picture, I can see them each day. What are the gifts in your life? The expected and unexpected ones. How closely do you have to look? Is it your home, spouse, children, job, friends, a prized possession, hobbies, dreams, events, or learning experiences? Each of us has received many gifts in our lives, no matter what angle we look at it. The question is, do you look? Do you truly look at your life and see not only how it has changed from your younger years, but how you have changed your dreams based on experience, decisions, opportunities, or things you have learned from others?

Life never ends up the way we expect it to, does it? Hopefully we become better because of our lives and recognize the gifts that have come our way. Sometimes those gifts arrive in forms beyond recognition. But in time, like a caterpillar finds its way out of its cocoon, we allow ourselves to open up to the beautiful gift of the butterfly that has been bestowed on our quickly-spun, glazed-over life.

Here's hoping you see the butterfly in today. If not, may you see the caterpillar, which in time will bring the gift, perhaps an unexpected gift to build on for your life's dreams.

New Life Changes Everything

Those who have children or grandchildren easily understand that new life changes everything. The anticipation and arrival of a child can make us giddy, nervous, scared, and overprotective. It often recalls the things of our own childhood we wish not to repeat while complementing those we want to continue to make part of this new life.

Since I do not have children or grandchildren of my own, I have relied on those I have known in these precious times of life. As a Children, Youth and Family Pastor I have had many opportunities to be around pregnant women, infants, young children, and their families. The entire family unit shifts when a new life is growing in its mother's womb. Each person has its own dreams and hopes for this new life. One of the first questions asked of this new child's family is, "Do you want a boy or a girl, a brother or a sister?" We ask their preference to begin a conversation about their initial dreams for this child. These hopes and dreams often suggest our own desire to inflict what we find important on this new child in our life. When my older brother, who was two, was asked if he wanted a little sister or brother, he responded that he didn't care as long as it was orange, which set into play his two year old priority for life. Everything needed to revolve around his favorite color. As long as it was orange, he was happy.

The new life which had the greatest impact on my life was that of my niece. My brother and I were married a couple of years apart and early in our marriages neither of us had children. I had two step-children the moment I said "I do," but I didn't have the opportunity to know and love them before they were born or during their early years of life. My brother and his wife had difficulty conceiving a child, and there was a time I wondered if my parents would ever have grandchildren. I had known for a long time that I would not have children of my own, but I never dreamed that God would take my brother down the same road.

We gathered one Christmas at my parents' home to celebrate the holidays. My parents made arrangements for us to have family portraits taken. Toward the end of our holiday visit, I began to think something was very different with my sister-in-law. Initially I couldn't pinpoint what it was. After returning home I had a deep sense that she might be pregnant, but I didn't say a word. Over the years this had become a difficult topic of conversation and I did not want to cause more pain. Several weeks later Bill answered the phone, and it was my brother and sister-in-law. Bill quickly told me they wanted me on the phone too. As I walked across the room toward the phone I motioned a big belly to him, asking if they were going to tell us she was indeed pregnant. To my intense and overwhelming delight, that is exactly what they told us. The baby was expected to be born the end of September.

My excitement was great from the moment they told us. My only disappointment was that we lived in the Midwest and they lived in California, as did my parents. I lived so far from this new life that was growing quickly. I was overwhelmed with gratitude to God for this amazing gift. As any soon to be, first time aunt, I quickly immersed myself in all that was baby. I eagerly bought neutral colored clothes and toys, and anytime I went to the store I had to stop by the baby section, just in case there was something that stood out and called my name. Bill learned quickly not ask where I was going, and if we got split up in a store he knew exactly where to find me – the baby section! I was having the time of my life.

One day out of nowhere it hit me. The what if's began. What if something went wrong? What if this little one wasn't healthy? These are the questions any soon-to-be parent asks. As this child's aunt, these questions hit me really hard. This was the first time in my life I felt guilty for my disease because I truly didn't know if this new baby would have any of the physical or medical challenges I had faced. I didn't want my brother and sister-in-law to be faced with such a situation, and I felt responsible. None of us would know the answers to these questions until we could lay our eyes on this tiny one. Internally I was a mess as my concern for this new little life grew stronger with each day. The only place I could take these concerns was to God.

Sometime that spring, we learned that this baby was a little girl. I would have a niece. The shopping became more specific as did the dreams and hopes. A short time later my greatest disappointment with the news of this new life became much less of an issue. I received a call to be the Youth and Family Pastor at a congregation in Arizona. Southern California and Phoenix, Arizona are much closer in proximity than Minneapolis, Minnesota and Southern California. I even had the opportunity to join a work force that met more than four times a year in a community near where my brother and his family lived. I would get to see my niece more than I ever dreamed.

Over a year before all of this excitement began, I had made the decision to grow out my hair with the intent of donating it to make wigs for those who faced medical challenges and lost their hair. I decided to have my hair cut the day before the baby shower in honor of this new life we were celebrating. I had 12 inches of hair cut and donated it to Locks of Love. Locks of Love is a public non-profit organization that provides hairpieces to financially disadvantaged children under age 21 suffering from long-term medical hair loss from any diagnosis. What an honor it was to say thanks to God for this new little girl by donating my hair to someone who really needed to be blessed in this way. The baby shower took place on my birthday. I was more than delighted to turn the focus from my birthday to celebrating my little niece who would soon be in our arms.

Before the party, my brother and sister-in-law offered me the two most incredible gifts anyone could ever give. What a surprise this was as I never imagined being more excited for her arrival than I already was. They gave me a card and gift to open. In all honesty I don't even remember what was inside the gift bag as the most important gifts were the words written in the card. The card was actually from my niece and the front said; "Happy Birthday, Godmother." They were asking me to play an active role in her spiritual life. I knew I couldn't be her Godmother, because she would be baptized in the Catholic Church. I could however be her Christian Sponsor. In all reality, for the purposes of spiritual support and direction, they were the same. What an honor. The second gift was how the card was signed. In most situations, the salutation and signature at the end of a letter or card don't mean that much. On this day, my life changed. Not only was I going to be my niece's Godmother but she would be my namesake. The birthday wishes were signed "Love, Hailey Kristine." My niece was going to be named after me.

I returned home immediately after the baby shower as I had to preach that weekend. My heart was full of love, joy, and excitement. My heart sang and anyone who saw me knew it. As the days grew closer to her expected birth date, my excitement grew. My parents made plans that as soon as my sister-in-law went into labor, they would drive down to meet their granddaughter. Most likely, she would arrive into this world before they arrived at the hospital. I had given my parents specific instructions to call me as soon as they received word that she was on her way. I didn't care what time it was. Day or night, they were to call me. Very early on a Monday morning my mom called and said they were on their way to the hospital and in several hours they would not only have arrived but hoped to be holding their first grandchild. With this news, I requested they call with any updates they received.

The moment I hung up the phone, fear crept in. I did not feel the guilt I felt early on in her development, this time I felt fear. Fear of the unknown and what would happen if something was wrong with this sweet little girl. I knew it could be hours before I heard anything. I was still hundreds of miles away, so I did the only thing I could do at the moment to make a difference: I prayed. I initially prayed for my sister-in-law, my niece, my brother, my parents and their traveling, and the doctors and nurses. Then I remembered that God already knew how this day would end and it meant He wasn't going anywhere. If God was there, we could handle anything that came our way today with His help. So these prayers of concern turned into prayers of gratitude. I prayed prayers of gratitude until the phone rang again. Hailey Kristine had arrived, and all was well. Yes, all was well. Once again God had proven that my guilt, fear, and concern had become useless energy. It was so clear to me that having a heart of gratitude was much more productive than the negative alternative.

I received a lot of pictures through email and snail mail. I plastered her pictures all over my desk and office. I wanted everyone to know what God had just done! This was yet another miracle. A little over a month later, I would have my chance to take my own pictures and hold this precious bundle of joy. Family and friends would travel near and far to celebrate her baptism. I would stand up for her and offer prayers as we presented her to God as a new child in His family. What a glorious day it was.

There was yet another gift I was given: I was able to stay with this sweet little girl the first days her mother went back to work. I had babysat for numerous families when I was a teenager, but this was very different. My heart was different. As I sat alone with her that week I wrote these words: "She is too beautiful for words. My heart stops beating just so I can use all of my being to absorb her. Tiny little nose, ears, lips, and eyes bluer than the ocean. She depends on so much, but provides even more."

I had learned that the amount one relies on another doesn't always compare equally to their ability to give. At this time in her life, she relied on others for her every need. In return she gave infinitely more than she received. This was God's design. This tiny being gave love, peace, hope, and joy simply by being present. She had touched the depth of my being forever.

Almost three years later, my nephew was born. I now had two little ones to bring me infinite joy. Just picturing them in my mind could turn a terribly difficult situation with tears into smiles and laughter. This became a new coping mechanism for me in their early years of life. When my life was chaotic and difficult, I would imagine their giggles in my mind and everything changed. I had a sense of hope again.

The day my nephew was baptized I encountered a new emotion. He was baptized in a charismatic Roman Catholic Church. As my brother and sister-in-law stood with his Godparents at the baptismal font they made a decision which affected me in a way I never expected. By this time in my life I had witnessed hundreds of baptisms and officiated at more than I could count. The ceremony was not new to me in the slightest. As the priest spoke the words so familiar to me, my sister-in-law and my nephew's Godmother did something unexpected by everyone in the church. They took all of my nephew's clothes off. He would be completely submerged in the waters of baptism. This is not very common in the background I was raised, but I had read enough and seen it on television. The impact of this event was substantial. As he was lifted up high by the priest he was offered to God with his entire being. It was the only thing he could offer at the time. As he was lowered into the water everyone in the room took a deep breath and as he was raised out of the water we exhaled loudly. As cries of my nephew rang through the church I was overwhelmed with the emotion of this experience. When he gasped for air it felt as if he breathed in every ounce of what God was offering for his life. This tiny child came before God with nothing but himself to offer and as he was raised out of the water he gasped for air with new life in the family of God.

New life certainly does change everything. Whether it is the birth of a child or the rebirth of one into the family of God, everything is changed in the blink of an eye. Once we are a part of the family, our job is to help care for those who are younger than we are or are not capable of caring for themselves. We are to tell and retell the stories of the family so this new member knows where they came from. Consistency over time truly tells the story. My job with my niece and nephew is to not only tell our familial stories, but also the stories of our faith. In order for them to say they are a part of either family, they must know the stories and know where they fit into them. I want them to know the all-important story of hope, forgiveness, love, and acceptance. In the eyes of God they have a lot to give. After all, I want the depth of their beings to be touched as mine was. I want them to be claimed by the story of Good News, the story of health and wellbeing, the story of grace, hope, and love. It is only then that they can keep telling and retelling the story – the story which reminds us that new life really does change everything.

Everyone Can Change a Life

Life is a peculiar thing. When I look back on those who have come in and out of my life, there are numerous interactions which have made a deep impact on me. The interesting thing about these people and the interactions we shared is that they are not that spectacular in the grand scheme of life. They are simple, ordinary acts that have made me think a little harder or differently, brought a smile to my face, and settled deep in my soul.

One of the important components to these interactions is to understand that they are not bound by age, economy, or education. In fact, most of them come from the brilliant minds of children. I love it when a child speaks and I am stopped dead in my tracks to ponder, laugh, or say, "Why didn't I think of that?" In all reality, to make an impact on the life of another person you don't need much. You need an honest and open heart that isn't intimidated by those around you. From there you speak or observe the mighty gifts of God. It is as simple as that. When God is allowed to speak through us, nothing inhibits us. Enjoy the following glimpses of how my life has been blessed by the presence of God in the lives of one family.

In my faith tradition most people are baptized as an infant or child. Yes, adults are baptized, but it is a rare occasion. To make it even more rare, many adult baptisms take place during private ceremonies. When I was serving a large congregation as the Pastor of Youth and Family Ministry, I had the privilege to officiate at an adult baptism which stands out beyond all baptisms I had conducted. Before I tell you about the baptism, here's some background information.

~Todd was a gentle, married man and father of three. He was an active businessman who hunted and fished and loved to be with his family. His wife, Dana, had begun to attend church with the children. One spring day she asked Todd to join her for a study at church one night a week for several weeks. Free childcare was provided! Todd thought, "Time with my wife, away from the kids and free childcare - how can I lose?" Todd did not expect to leave this study a changed man. He learned about the love and grace of God in a way he had never imagined. For the first time in his life he was understanding more about this God his wife and children were so excited about. In addition, during this time Todd's mother came to live with him and his family. It was toward the end of her life. During this time, Todd learned he had been dedicated as a child, but had not been baptized.

The study gnawed at Todd's soul and threw him quickly into a conversation with me about getting baptized. Todd did not want to be like the other adults. He was proud of his new life in Christ and wanted everyone in our church to witness and be a part of his new journey as a baptized believer. In addition, he wanted his family to be actively involved in his baptism because they were a large part of what brought him back to Christ. Together we gathered his entire family and proceeded to make arrangements. By now, Todd's family was very active in many different aspects of church life. This made planning his baptism enjoyable for all. The oldest, Amy, read Scripture and a welcoming text that is a part of our liturgy. Their middle child and only son, Doug, then the quietest of the three, kept a special prayer rock in his pocket and held the baptismal napkin. He did a perfect job. Then there was the youngest and most vivacious personality, Tara. From the moment we began to plan the baptism, the only thing Tara wanted to do was pour the water from the pitcher to the font. Tara had paid close attention during worship and knew without a doubt that water was a very important part of any baptism. Without water, there was no baptism. So at the appropriate time, Tara and I both poured the water into the font.

This joyous event began a new life in Christ for Todd. His faith and family took on new meaning. Priorities changed. The children asked more questions and with each question there was much more to learn. Because Todd now understood the importance of the church community's presence at his baptism he was able to teach the congregation that they have a role beyond the few sentences of support and welcome they speak during the ceremony. Todd taught them that the church community is the larger family and we are all to take responsibility for each other and help out, because that is what families do. The stories that follow revolve around Todd and Dana's three children. The head of their household was now a true man of God who wanted his family to experience Jesus personally, which they did and continue to do.

~Amy is an intelligent young woman. She has a heart that is passionate for helping others and learning. She has taken part in Mission trips, taught Sunday School and Vacation Bible School, and been a camp counselor. For many Christian denominations Lent is a time to prepare hearts and reflect on our lives as we look toward the death and resurrection of Jesus. We are given a great gift by God during this time, and one way to draw closer to God is to change something in our lives. In many congregations it is common to hear the words, "What are you going to give up for Lent?" Sometimes people choose give up their most cherished food or a lifestyle choice. Another approach is to add something to life that will draw a person closer to God. Whether a person is giving up or adding something, the purpose is to be closer to God by the end of Lent. This makes for an even more glorious Easter celebration, because then celebrating Jesus's resurrection truly comes from the heart and soul.

Just before Lent one year at the age of nine, Amy presented her parents with a challenge: each of them had to read the Scripture reading in church during worship sometime during Lent. Amy's challenge went beyond Lent as she wanted to add it to their annual gifts to the church. Amy was comfortable reading out loud in public, but mom and dad were another story. One of the most feared things in the world is public speaking, and Amy's parents were no different. In all reality though, Amy had a good point: the study of Scripture weeks before they were to read publically would definitely allow God's word to be more present in their lives. In addition, it would allow them to discuss more Scripture in their home as they struggled with some meanings and pronunciations. God tugged at Amy's heart and Amy accepted the challenge. As God planned all along, this Lenten commitment became a faith commitment as they continued to find new ways to learn and serve in the years to come.

-Doug had a quiet side to him when he was young. When comfortable and safe, he embraced many things with joy and contemplation. Doug had a gentle heart that could make anyone smile. In an earlier chapter I shared how during a hospitalization the kids returned from camp to encourage my recovery. Doug was not quite four and too young to be at camp that week, so he, his mother and sisters visited me in the hospital several times. During one of the visits, Doug presented me with the sweetest stuffed teddy bear, which he named "Teddy." His thoughtful, gentle heart wanted to remind me that I was not alone and that God was with me. Doug was certain the bear would help in a similar way. He was right. Many months passed and Doug had his own medical difficulties. At this time, Doug still had a shy personality, even with those he knew quite well. One day I sat down with Doug and gave him Teddy to borrow back. At first he would have nothing to do with this, but after further conversation he was open to the possibility. I told Doug Teddy had served a great purpose for me at a frightening and lonely time. I thought Teddy could offer him some encouragement, friendship, and a safety net to fall on. Doug agreed to take Teddy, but only temporarily, because Teddy was mine. A gift and simple gesture served a greater purpose for both of us. Doug and I had future opportunities to share Teddy between us as we each endured difficulties and extra support was welcomed.

~Then there is Tara. Tara, the youngest of the family has a lively (sometimes edgy) personality, speaks her mind, makes people laugh and gives her all to sharing God with others. At the age of three, Tara was standing with two younger girls in front of a statue of Jesus located in our church entryway. Tara pointed to the statue and said, "That's Jesus, and we need to pray to Him." Tara then took their hands and thanked Jesus for His love. Tara did not comprehend the magnitude of God's love at that moment, but she knew she was supposed to pray to Jesus and share Him with others, no matter who they were or where they were. So, share she did.

~Tara was blessed with a giving spirit. Her mother was wise, and when they prepared to attend worship as a family, a snack bag was put together for Tara. This bag served more than one purpose; feed a hungry child and reign in an energetic personality just a little. Tara's mom was not aware that this simple snack would prove to have a greater purpose. During worship there is a time to offer God's peace to each other. Most people shake hands while others may share a hug, kiss, or a wave. Tara took sharing the peace of God a bit further and after shaking hands with others she would share from her snack bag. She wanted everyone to have the same opportunity she had.

~Our church offered Holy Communion a couple of times a month when people could reflect, draw closer to God, and remember the life-giving gifts Jesus gave to God's people when He died on the cross. Our church, not unlike other Christian churches, suggested an age when a person could receive communion after attending a class. Throughout my career I have been very involved in the education of Holy Communion. At this time in my parish ministry we offered such a class to second graders and their parents. This did not suggest that all second graders could comprehend the magnitude of this gift from God, but it was a time to begin and encourage their learning process. Holy Communion is one of the greatest gifts Jesus gave to us. It is a gentle reminder that we are never alone and are loved even when we feel messed up and confused. I have known adults who never come close to comprehending what Holy Communion is all about and I have known two year olds who have a clearer and more grace-filled understanding than most adults in our churches ever will. Tara was one of those who was wise beyond her years as she continually listened, learned, and practiced.

All are welcome to come before the altar to pray and receive either communion or a verbal blessing. In all reality, communion is just that, a blessing. Like most young children, Tara would come to the altar with her parents. Tara would stand, not kneel, so she could see everything that was taking place. Tara waited patiently for me to come and offer her mom and dad communion and give her a special blessing. Each time, week after week, Tara would then give me a Cheerio, imitating the way I had given her parents and most adults a tiny wafer to eat. Tara was mimicking Holy Communion. Tara knew this was a gift to be shared, so in her own way, she shared God as a gift from her tiny hands. She didn't utter a word, but her face said it all: "This is a gift for you. You can't earn it because it comes from my heart." My heart melted as Jesus lived in Tara, and I was a recipient of His love through her.

⁓Our church encouraged children and youth to take on leadership roles and be active in all areas of the church community. During worship it was not uncommon for a smaller child to assist an older sibling or parent in ushering duties. Included in this was the receiving of the offering. During one service Tara decided she did not want to help someone bigger than her, she wanted to usher and receive the offering all by herself. Her little feet carried her throughout our large worship space. Those attending were scattered all over the sanctuary and Tara thought this made her job more important as she went individually to each person. A man sat in the very last row all by himself. It was almost as if he was in a building by himself as he was at least ten rows away from any other person. When Tara arrived at the last pew, she placed the offering basket in front of the man. The man shook his head, motioning to Tara that he was not going to contribute. Tara thought this was very odd as she was taught that when the offering basket is put in front of you money is placed inside, no matter how small your gift. Tara then shook her head in response, and pushed the basket again toward the man. Again the man shook his head more vigorously telling Tara that he did not intend to give an offering. One last time Tara pushed the basket back toward the man and he reached deep into his pocket and placed an offering in the basket. I understand that the man may have had many reasons as to why he did not intend on giving an offering that night, but Tara would hear nothing of it. To Tara, when we have the opportunity to thank God - with our money or otherwise - we thank God, always. Tara is able to challenge others in a way that most people cannot get away with. I believe that God led her tiny feet that night to tug at the heart of a man who thought he could go to church and no one, not even God would know he was there. Tara wanted him to know that she knew he was there, and if she knew then surely God knew too.

~Halloween is a very popular secular holiday. It seems each year decorations are available for purchase earlier and earlier. Many Christian churches have been turned off by Halloween and the scary, ghoulish, violent nature it can take on. The curve has gone so far that many churches will not embrace the All Souls celebration which was common for the early church. Early in the 21st Century, churches and communities sought an alternative to the Halloween many families wanted to celebrate. Trunk or Treat came into being, a combination of Trick or Treating and a Fall Harvest Festival. It is a time when those who wished could dress up, play games, and receive candy as it was passed out from the trunks of decorated cars in a safe church parking lot and feast on hot apple cider, fun size candy bars, caramel apples, and popcorn.

Most children dress up in the latest cartoon character that has been plastered over every medium possible. Some revert back to a favorite Disney character, animal, clown, princess, or pumpkin. It seems that each year there is one costume that appears more times than I can count. I remember one year when Harry Potter came to my door ten times in an evening, and it was a different child each time. One year in particular, Amy, Doug, and Tara took great courage and care in selecting their costumes. They each arrived in a one of a kind costume. Amy and Doug came in unique costumes that fit the event and I doubt no one in the state of Minnesota had a similar costume. Tara on the other hand had a one of a kind, once in a lifetime costume. Amy arrived dressed as Mary, the mother of Jesus. Mary is an important part of the Christian story and Amy wanted Mary to be a name that was appreciated for the difficult journey her life took on when God sent an angel to tell her she would be the mother of God's son. Doug took on a boyhood excitement when he learned that living the life of a Christian may be difficult at times and may call for one to engage in battle. The battle God calls His children to is much different than a war in which people die a meaningless death. God calls His children to put on the Full Armor of God in order to survive the Christian life in the world we must live.

> *Finally, be strong in the Lord and in the strength of his power. Put on the whole armor of God, so that you may be able to stand against the wiles of the devil. For our struggle is not against enemies of blood and flesh, but against the rulers, against the authorities, against the cosmic powers of this present darkness, against the spiritual forces of evil in the heavenly places. Therefore take up the whole armor of God, so that you may be able to withstand on that evil day, and having done everything, to stand*

firm. Stand therefore, and fasten the belt of truth around your waist, and put on the breastplate of righteousness. As shoes for your feet put on whatever will make you ready to proclaim the gospel of peace. With all of these, take the shield of faith, with which you will be able to quench all the flaming arrows of the evil one. Take the helmet of salvation, and the sword of the Spirit, which is the word of God. (Ephesians 6:10-17, NRSV)

Doug was adorned with the full armor spoken of in Ephesians. He had saved his money so he could buy a costume from our local Christian Bookstore. The armor was complete with belt, breastplate, shoes, shield, helmet, and sword. I would choose to have Doug with me anytime I struggle against evil, for he understands God's direction.

Tara's creation made this particular Halloween celebration especially unforgettable for me. It was a first and most certainly will be my last. Tara arrived in a self-created costume wearing her long white bathrobe with a green towel hanging forward on her neck, a large cross that hung to her belly button, the hands free microphone adapter from their home phone, carrying her Bible. Tara dressed up as me on Sunday morning! During worship we pastors used headpiece microphones like that of pop stars. One afternoon a few weeks before Halloween, Tara was walking through their house singing Sunday School songs, wearing her white bathrobe, and the microphone headpiece. Her mom asked what she was doing and she said she was "playing Pastor Kris." Her costume bloomed from there. I knew we had a good relationship, but I never knew the role model I had become for the nearly four year old Tara until that day.

~I have always been impressed by the openness and willingness of Amy, Doug, and Tara to ask questions as God placed them in their hearts. Whether in the middle of church, the middle of the night, a long car ride, or the dinner table, they continually pondered God and sought a deeper understanding of Him. One day Amy noted the Bible was a heavy book. She continued by stating, "It's a good thing that Jesus died on the cross in order to forgive our sins, because if our sins were not forgiven, the Bible would be too heavy for us to carry with all of our sins still inside." Many days Doug would race up to me with the question of the day and his mom or dad would smile and say, "Sorry, I couldn't answer that one so we saved it for you." I have always felt it is very important that questions about God and faith be raised by all. I have never claimed to have all the answers, or even most of them, but I will seek to learn more as I search for various answers.

In the midst of our learning we each have our own understanding of God's expectations. Tara is no different. One morning I was reading to the congregation the Scripture verses I would soon preach on. I stood several steps up in the pulpit. Tara sat in the second row with her family. It is important to note that I find it vitally helpful for families with young children to sit toward the front of any event. Children are adventurous and inquisitive. The closer they are to the action, the more they learn and the more they will feel a part of whatever is going on. For me, church is no different. Their family took time to learn the importance of this lesson. Perhaps Tara's words on this noted day delayed their learning, perhaps out of sheer embarrassment. The text I read came from the book of Matthew:

> *"...for I was hungry and you gave me food, I was*
> *thirsty and you gave me something to drink, I was*

*a stranger and you welcomed me, I was naked
and you gave me clothing, I was sick and you took
care of me, I was in prison and you visited me."
(Matthew 25:35-36, NRSV)*

I barely said the third word in verse 36 when Tara blurted loudly
for all to hear, "Pastor Kris said naked in church (giggle, giggle,
giggle)!" Her parents wanted to hide and everyone else tried very
hard to keep their laughter contained so that I could read the rest
of the Scripture. Sure it is funny but there is a bigger picture here.
This reminds me that we must be so careful in what we say and
do, at all times. This is a time in our worship service when we tend
to believe that the children, if not the adults, are paying attention
to something else because they are bored or have no chance at
comprehending what is going on. Obviously this isn't so. Tara was
paying very careful attention. Word for word she knew what was
being said so much that it didn't make sense to be said in church.
After all, how many times do we say the word "naked" anyway?
So be careful, because you never know who is listening, watching,
or absorbing everything you say and do.

~Most adults will say that they feel older when the children in
their lives hit specific milestones in life. When in the seventh
grade, Tara was assigned to write a paper on what she was good
at. Tara struggled at first for a starting point. She then decided to
turn to her church family for ideas. Not many youth will claim
their faith while attending a public school. Read Tara's thoughts,
"A Servant's Heart."

*"Everyone can be great because anyone can serve.
You don't have to have a college degree to serve. You
don't even have to make your subject and your verb*

agree to serve... You only need a heart full of grace.
A soul generated by love..."

Dr. Martin Luther King, Jr.

When we got this assignment, I wasn't sure what to write about, so I asked my church family what they thought. Most of their responses were "Oh my goodness! You've been able to run our church since you were seven! You're amazing at serving God and other people." I love taking time out of my day to help others, and to do that, I go on mission trips, create fundraisers, run carnivals, pack care packages, work at the food shelf or shelter, cook meals for my church, and much more!

As I have grown up my family has been super involved in our church. By the age of six I could run the whole industrial kitchen by myself, and by the time I was seven I was practically on the church council. I walk around talking to people, and the adults ask me to teach them how to run the dishwasher, or turn the hose in the sink on. Every Sunday I am doing something; working in the kitchen, running the nursery, teaching Sunday school, leading the kids worship, ushering, lighting the candles and helping the pastors, or serving communion.

I have learned that serving also has its downfalls. There are times I can't go to a friend's house because I have plans to be somewhere else, serving. I fed the homeless this winter during a snowstorm and my friends wanted me join them for an epic snowball fight, but I didn't join them because I was serving. When I went out of town to run a kids club for children without a safe place to go, my friends wanted me to go swimming with them, but I didn't because I was serving. When I stayed overnight at church raising money to feed kids in Africa by fasting for 30 hours, my friends wanted to have a sleepover and make Mickey Mouse pancakes, but I was serving, so I didn't go.

To me, serving is a time to forget about everything that is going on around me, and focus on the people I'm helping. Every time that I serve I turn off my cell phone so that I am not distracted. If you have distractions, you can't make as big of an impact on the people you're serving. I also love to hear their stories. You can learn a lot from others. Even if I hear the same story day after day I still learn something new each time I heard it because I am there for God.

I've always been told that faith the size of a mustard seed will move mountains. When I serve, I can see in people's eyes that little bit of faith growing inside them, and I know that with a little more faith, they will move mountains. We have the power to give them the mustard seed.

When my ministry ended at this congregation, it was very difficult for me to leave for many reasons. This family was one of those reasons. I have a very special item that was given to me by Tara before I moved to the other side of the country. Tara handed me an envelope and told me to keep it safe. Once I got home I opened it to find a three inch chunk of her platinum blonde hair with a note in her handwriting, "so you won't forget me." Later that year I sent Tara a similar envelope and note with a section of my hair which was cut to donate to Locks of Love.

Amy saw things differently than any of us when I was about to move. God gave her the gift of taking her emotions out of the situation and teaching the adults how to trust God's plan. Amy was talking to her mom and said they should not be sad because I was going to a place that God was leading. Amy likened the situation to Jesus and Peter before Jesus was put to death. Jesus knew His death had to happen because of God's plan and there was no use in arguing about it. Amy saw my move for a new ministry the same way; if God was calling me to move and minister elsewhere then how could they argue about it? They had to support me in my journey and pray for God's continued blessing. I would love to say that I had a great influence on this family, but the fact is they impacted my life in more ways that I can count or ever comprehend.

It is again a reminder to me that we may be the only opportunity someone has to learn about God. If we stay connected to God through prayer, the study of Scripture, and the larger community, we can always do something to honor God. No one can do it alone, but if we each take small steps, God's word and love will be spread out to others who need to know that they are loved unconditionally. We never know where God may need us. We are told to come to God as little children. The leaders are told in Scripture not to hinder or hold back the children from God.

> *Jesus said, "Let the little children come to me, and do not stop them; for it is to such as these that the kingdom of heaven belongs." (Matthew 19:14, NRSV)*

I have taken this demand by Jesus seriously. Children have a right to know Jesus! When Jesus says we are to come as a child, He is not limiting this to those under ten years of age. Jesus is directing it to those who are young or limited in the faith. Each of us is there at some point in life. As life's journey moves on, and learning situations become a part of our present, it is not uncommon for us to sway back to our early days and need encouragement for our faith. This is why we need to be present for each other. God puts others on this earth to help us through the hard times, build us up when we are down, bring us joy when we are sad, and shed a tear when we are hurt. Once we learn to do this, we teach others through our words and actions.

Amy, Doug, and Tara continue to be witnesses to God's powerful word. Their entire beings have: challenged others to do what is right; brought comfort and love to those who are sick; been an avenue for giving; witnessed to God's amazing word; questioned with insight and without fear; and served as the hands and feet of God. They are truly a gift from God, and I am privileged to continue to learn from them.

The Story My
Parents Told Me

My story cannot be told without looking deeply into the thoughts, feelings, and experiences of my parents. The feelings my parents have experienced since my birth have been varied and complex. When I reflect upon my own feelings I often find myself imagining what it was - and is - like for them. I am often brought to tears when considering the love they have for me. Since I am not a mother myself, I can only imagine the love a parent has for his/her own child(ren). It is only then that I am able to slightly comprehend the love my parents have for me.

My mom and dad each have their own recollections of life before I was born. They each had their own expectations and feelings about my impending birth. My dad in particular recalls that he and my mom were at a time in their lives where things were good. All that they had planned was going well. They had been married for six years, had a two and a half year old son, recently bought their first home, and had a new car. My dad enjoyed his job with the possibility of ongoing promotions.

Both my mom and dad were a part of a study group at church. As they got to know others in their group they discovered others were dealing with the difficulties of death, divorce, and problems with children. My parents talked to each other about how they didn't have issues like the others and wondered if they were out of place. For both my mom and dad, life was as good as they could remember. One night my dad mentioned to my mom that he wondered if this could be the lull before the storm.

When my mom first learned she was pregnant with me she was thankful and overjoyed that she was finally pregnant. She was also concerned because she had been very sick before she found out that she was pregnant. She tells a story of a day while pregnant with me, when she took my brother to the park so he could have some fun. She also hoped she might tire him out a bit as any pregnant mom of a toddler might do. While they were there, she saw a little boy with very short arms. She pondered how difficult life must be for him. On the other hand, it stood out to her that he was smiling, having fun, and playing like the other children. She stopped to say a little prayer for him. Little did she know that this little boy would end up being an inspiration to her sometime after I was born. He was a little angel, a messenger from God, saying, "Look at me, I'm okay, and she will be too."

The emotion surrounding the day a child is born is typically great for anyone, no matter the situation. My parents entered this day with great expectations and joy. They had taken my brother to a neighbor's house and arrived at the hospital by 5:00 a.m. I was born just before 6:00 a.m. My mom was filled with overflowing joy and thanksgiving the moment I was born when the nurse said, "She has a pretty little face" and whisked me away to an incubator. Like with my brother, my mom was not allowed to hold me right after I was born. My dad was told everything was fine and to go get some rest. He got a couple of hours sleep, picked up my brother, and started making phone calls to family and close friends.

Before my dad arrived back at the hospital, the pediatrician went to speak to my mom. The first words out of her mouth were, "What kind of drugs did you take?" My mom told her she only took the medication her doctor had ordered. This doctor then informed my mom that I was born with multiple birth defects. My mom was devastated, disappointed, and filled with grief. This grief was not just for her but for me and what would possibly be ahead for all of us. At the same time my mom was angry with her obstetrician, as he had said nothing to her or my dad that morning to give them a reason to believe anything was wrong. She lay in her bed wondering how she was going to tell my dad.

Shortly after noon my dad picked up a dozen roses and went back to the hospital. Instead of finding a happy and joyful wife, he found her sobbing. My mom doesn't recall how she told him the news. My dad doesn't recall how far she got telling him about all of my problems before he became numb. This was not what either of them expected for this day and they had no idea how to cope. The day ended with feelings of guilt, anger, resentment, helplessness, and fear of the unknown. They wondered what resources were available to help them travel the difficult road they now traveled. They asked, "Why?"

God provided all the resources necessary not only to survive but to thrive. My mom describes it as God revealing a little bit at a time, to help us as a family cope. It was a blessing not to know everything when I was born that we now know about my disease. Initially my parents' dreams for a healthy baby were turned upside down. Their Christian friends were very supportive. They would take care of my brother and provide emotional and spiritual support for my parents. These friends were there at the drop of a hat for whatever was needed. There also were those who were not supportive and didn't really know what to say or how to help my mom and dad. This included those who told them they must have done something terrible for their baby to have been born with all these defects. Then there were the ones who told my parents they didn't have enough faith and belief in God to take away all of my problems. Before my fourth birthday, my parents were told that I was expected to die before I completed high school. My parents decided not to tell anyone – not even me - this information. At one time my mom and dad were told by some of the medical staff how some families deal with children born like me in some foreign countries. They were told parents take their less-than-perfect children to the edge of town and leave them there to die. My parents knew that even though there were more questions than answers, they were not alone: God was with them. He gave them the strength they needed to face all that was before them.

One of the amazing gifts God provided that both of my parents recall, is their weak and strong moments were opposite each other. They were each given exactly the strength they needed as a couple to overcome the current hurdle and move onto the next one. My mom found it stressful and difficult each time she would take me to the doctor for tests and surgeries. My dad on the other hand was more matter of fact dealing with what needed to be done up to the point I was put on the gurney and taken to the operating room. At that time my mom would take over and go as far with me as she was permitted, as my dad could not hold himself together. I never knew this until my adult years. I always thought only one of them was permitted to join me on the route to surgery. My dad also was very fortunate to have understanding bosses that never questioned his need to be absent the day of my surgeries or for important doctor appointments.

When I was two months old we traveled to Orthopedic Hospital in Los Angeles where we had been referred to for information and hopefully some direction. It was a two-hour drive from our home to the hospital. When they left the house they felt as though they had the world on their shoulders. When they returned home they felt more thankful and fortunate that my medical problems were not more extensive. During our first trip to the hospital clinic I went through many different tests and had more than 20 x-rays taken. After meeting with variety of doctors all day, my parents were swimming with information and confusion. They were told I had boney abnormalities and numerous types of tumors, some of which could not be diagnosed. It was expected that many of the tumors would disappear by the time I was five years of age. The tumors never disappeared and continue to grow today. When the day was over all they knew was that this was going to involve a lot of doctor appointments, tests, and surgeries. When we left the hospital we had many more appointments scheduled, and it was pretty obvious that this was a life-changing event for us all. It definitely wasn't going to be a quick and easy fix.

Preparing for the trip home, we arrived in the hospital parking lot and my dad gave my mom the car keys asking her to drive home. This took place at 4:00 p.m. in downtown Los Angeles. My dad told her that this was going to be a long road ahead of us with many trips to the hospital and he couldn't take off work every time I had an appointment. She had to get used to making this drive by herself. I can only imagine her fear since she had only obtained her driver's license when she was pregnant with me. My mom continues to be amazed at the protection God offered during the countless trips to the hospital and clinic throughout the years. These trips were before call boxes along the freeway and cell phones. We traveled a variety of different roads and freeways through Los Angeles including and because of the downtown traffic jams. We were kept safe each and every trip.

My parents faced a decision very early on that would influence the rest of my life: should they shelter me or put me out in the world? They chose to put me out in the world and not to hide me. When I was eight months old, my mom took me out to the other children in the neighborhood. She laid me on a blanket, wearing only my diaper and let the neighborhood children see and ask questions. She told them I was just as special as they were even though I looked very different. They talked about anything the children noticed from the tip of my head to the end of my very large toes. As the children pointed to some of my noticeable tumors my mom told them we called them "lumpy bumpies." This was an easy concept for my brother and later for me to understand. This decision to bring me out to the other children was seminal in my development. To this day I put myself "out there" and on the line. If a question is asked, I answer it with honesty.

At the age of two years old, a huge red ball of fire instantly appeared directly under my arm. This was my longest hospitalization of 27 days. Additional precautions were taken and I was placed in isolation. The huge red ball of fire turned out to be an infected lymphangioma. The doctors had no idea how to treat it. Their best idea was to start high doses of IV antibiotics. Fortunately this worked. The inflammation decreased and the infection went away. It was during times like these that we had to trust that God would provide the right answers to my physicians, because no one knew what might work. We continue to be thankful that my doctors never stopped searching for new and improved ways to treat my complex medical situation and taking the risks to do so. Throughout the years there have been more successful treatments than failed ones.

During this hospitalization I met the woman who would become my favorite doctor, Dr. Whiteman. She became my pediatrician for major events and hospitalizations. Dr. Whiteman also played an integral role in my care and coordinated with all of my specialists. No matter why I was hospitalized she would visit and make sure everything was taken care of. She learned early on that I was a very determined little girl with a lot of spunk. We developed a very special bond of mutual respect, almost a friendship. I recall her bringing me a beautiful scarf from her trip to China one year. She also encouraged my mom to bring jelly beans to the hospital and have me eat them before I went to sleep the night before my surgeries. I will never know if she really thought it would help my recovery or not. She had told us that the way my body would process the sugar of the jelly beans would also help how I processed the medications used during surgery. Perhaps it was her way of encouraging a positive tradition and coping mechanism in the midst of something difficult in life. She knew there would be numerous surgeries in my future. We always knew she was at the hospital by looking out the waiting room window into the employee parking lot. She drove a pick Cadillac with the license plate "Say Ah."

The hospital visits were all too frequent with numerous surgeries to follow. My parents kept track of the mileage for tax purposes. One year they logged more than 8,000 miles for just my appointments. This didn't include surgeries or the days they visited me in the hospital following each of my five surgeries that particular year. By the time I was eighteen, I had been through 25 operations. My parents only missed visiting me one day, which was during my longest hospitalization of 27 days.

We all learned to put our trust in the doctors and nurses, even when we knew they wouldn't always be right. There were times in which we needed to be vulnerable and trust them even though they didn't know what they were doing, as they had not faced some of my medical complications before. There were many firsts for everyone, doctors included. After numerous misdiagnoses, we came to understand that God was the only one who really knew everything that was going on in my body. Both of my parents felt the pain of making me do things that they knew would initially cause me pain. It was God's grace, strength, endurance, and hope that directed my parents to listen for God's guidance amidst the unknown and ever-changing direction and diagnoses throughout my life.

Throughout the years new technologies were developed and I had the opportunity to be among the first to receive some treatments society is familiar with today. I was one of the first to receive laser treatments. The laser was used to treat what my doctors thought were port-wine stains located on my trunk area. They bled often from their raised surface, like when a scab comes off too soon. When I was born doctors told us these would disappear by the time I turned five. This laser treatment was done while I was in high school. I had lived with the pain and inconvenience of these marks my entire life and we held hope for this new treatment. It was anticipated that this laser would not only smooth their surface but also lighten these marks to be barely noticeable. My mom was permitted to be with me during the procedure. The doctor proceeded without any type of pain medication or anesthesia. Part way through the first treatment, my mom couldn't take any more of the pain I was undergoing. She screamed, "Stop, stop! No more!" My pain was excruciating and she felt as if she just sat there and let the doctor continue. It hurt my mom to watch me suffer. In the end, the laser did lighten the marks somewhat, but they still bleed to this day. Later they were diagnosed as cavernous hemangiomas, and now I know them as vascular malformations, something that lasers cannot cure.

One type of tumor I am diagnosed with is called a lipoma. It is a benign, fat-like tumor. When liposuction first came out to help those with weight difficulties, or those who just wanted to shape their figure by removing smaller amounts of fat, my doctors believed it could be used for lipoma removal. Yes, I had liposuction. It seems kind of funny to say "I had lipo," especially since I am not too vain about my appearance. Unfortunately this treatment was not successful. The lipoma needed to be surgically removed through multiple, invasive operations.

God provided many opportunities for my parents to be surprised by my determination and creativity. I would overcome obstacles in my path that would make most people discouraged to the extent of giving up. They would watch me pick up tiny things with my thumb that pointed to my elbow and my middle finger, as a birth defect had made it impossible for me to do so normally. As a little girl I watched the neighbor girls head off to dance lessons. I too wanted to participate. Amazingly we were able to find shoes that we could force my feet into so I could attend tap dancing classes. I dreamt of dancing on the stage at our Valley Fair, and did so with my class.

My brother was a part of the track team. I loved to watch the events and thought that the distance runs looked like they were full of freedom. While in High School, I took part in Adaptive Physical Education. We did what everyone else did during PE, but it was adapted to what each of us could to with our own limitations. I remember heading to the track one day to run the mile. I felt the freedom I had anticipated while watching others run the long distances. My instructor was the track coach and encouraged me to try and run two miles that day. I completed the two miles. Yes I was slower than most, but I completed it. I was so excited. When I got home, I told my parents I wanted to join the track team and run the two mile. My parents and brother were shocked. My dream of running distance for the track team didn't last long and it was the closest I ever got to taking part in a team sport. But I was happy, and I tried.

I often watched my dad and brother wrestle and arm wrestle. I was jealous of the fun they had, but was always told to get out of the way so I wouldn't get hurt. One day, I insisted that my dad arm wrestle me. With great hesitation and a lot of winking between my parents and my brother, dad agreed. My dad and I knelt on opposite sides of the piano bench and set our pose. Before I knew it I had won - but he didn't let me win, as he had planned. In all honesty, I cheated. I was so excited that my dad would actually arm wrestle me, I started to pull on his arm before the start. In the process, I lifted his arm and crashed his elbow down on the wooden piano bench before I held his hand in the winning position. Fortunately my dad wasn't seriously injured, but this was a reminder again to my family that I wasn't going to be held back, no matter what.

In the fifth grade I kept up with my classmates including going to outdoor school for a week while in a body cast after my second spinal fusion. I wasn't about to miss out on this adventure: hiking, learning about the outdoors, campfires, skits, and lots of fun. Later that year when my cast was removed my surgeon asked me to bend over so he could see and feel how straight my back was now after the surgery. I asked him how far he wanted me to bend. He requested I bend over as far as I felt comfortable. Much to his surprise I bent and put my head on the floor without bending my knees. He was about to have a panic attack as he had just performed my second spinal fusion, permanently connecting 80% of my spine. In other words, I shouldn't have been able to bend that far. I heard him say "bend," and I simply asked "how far?"

My parents learned from me as others did. It became more than how I overcame the things in life that challenged me. They were inspired by the strength and purpose I found in life. In the midst of the struggles of life I challenged them to be brave and not complain. When I was ordained in the fall of 1997, Pastor Johnson preached and presented me for ordination. He reflected upon the words he spoke to my parents shortly after I was born. He painted a picture for all in attendance. As he and my parents stood looking into my crib, he said, "She will teach us much." Somehow God provided me with the opportunity to teach my parents about the heart of God.

It is evident that from the moment my mother learned of my multiple birth defects my life has been filled with times of being tired and inspired; being met by hurdles and overcoming them; faced with trials and miracles, falling and bouncing back up, loving and forgiving. I encountered times of pain and healing, disappointment and growth, being fearful and learning to trust, waiting and hoping. Every time I would surmount an obstacle my parents wondered if it was the last or if there would be more to follow. As time has shown, there is always something difficult to follow. My comfort is in knowing that I travel through the valleys with God's presence and love.

None of us truly knows what our life will be comprised of. We decided early on not to focus on the 'should have's, would have's, or could have's.' We never blamed God for how things turned out. We learned to find joy in serving others and offer God our thanksgiving and praise in spite of our own circumstances. These became our solid responses to life's difficulties, which kept our faith focused on the grace of God and the hope He has for our future.

There are no direct answers to the question why I was born the way I was. Although we believe there are a great many answers concerning what we can do with this kind of an event when it arises. We learned what love is: sharing in both the joy and the pain of another. Our God is a God who wills health, fullness of life, and joy for His children. He is also the God who will enter into the pain and the hurt when, for some reason, that wholeness fails us. He joins in the struggle and helps us discover what is present in the way of life and joy.

This has been a journey which God called me and my parents to travel together the moment of my conception. God works in mysterious ways. As my mom explained it, "Once again, because of the life of a child, we learned a lot about God and how He wants us to live a life of devotion to Him in all circumstances." My dad told me how much I have inspired him and so many others. One of his deepest desires is that I never lose my love of God and the ability to radiate what God tells me, in a still small voice, to my soul.

I have been challenged by the circumstances of my life as well as those closest to me. It is with intense gratitude that I try to comprehend the love my parents have for me. We have been through much in this life together. I truly believe that God hand-picked them for me and me for them. We needed something from each other as much as we needed to give something to each other. It all began with love. The rest is molded daily through our continued relationship and the life journey God has called us to.

Chosen to Love, Chosen to Care ~ words from Bill

I met Kris in the parking lot of Pacific Lutheran Theological Seminary on my very first day. I had heard that someone else arrived shortly before me also toting all their possessions in a U-haul moving van. I guess that was not a common occurrence for those who came to seminary in Berkeley, California in the past. Although I had not set out to find this person, God curiously would bring us together as we walked toward and greeted each other in that very parking lot. Little did I know that this was the beginning of an unexpected journey filled with blessings, growth, and challenges.

Pacific Lutheran is built on a hill, with the main buildings at the top and the dorms at the bottom. I was walking from the administration building after checking in and headed to my new room assignment. It was downhill. I would later come to really appreciate going that direction. As I was walking downhill back to the dorms, thinking about what the next two years would bring, a young lady greeted me about half way. She was small in stature and was coming from the dorms toward the administration building. This is a very steep and long uphill trek. She met me with a smile and a bubbly greeting of welcome. Kris was not shy! She asked me my name and whether I was attending school there.

It didn't take long into our conversation to discover we were the two who had come to seminary in moving vans. I also noticed that Kris seemed to be dealing with some physical challenges. However, one would not have known it from the effervescent personality, contagious smile, and total absence of acknowledging those challenges as she continued her way up the hill after our encounter. It seemed that with each step she took there was a joyful appreciation and spirit-filled love for being there.

What I did not realize or anticipate was the upcoming journey I was about to embark on. A few days later Kris would ask me if I could help her father set-up her new computer. Kris's dad, a bank vice-president, could approve million dollar loans, but all we could really say he knew about computers was how to turn them on and off. It took everything he had not to use that "garage" language. So I jumped in and got the computer set up and running. Kris and her mom were so thankful!

The weeks and months that followed were filled with deep theological discussions, either in the beautiful surroundings of the seminary, on long walks to see the lights of the San Francisco Bay at night, at Denny's for the Friday night all-you-can-eat shrimp, or at the local coffee shop drinking café mochas. We had many grand conversations with our fellow colleagues. None of these conversations, however, were deeper and more filled with the blessings of the Spirit than hearing someone's story lived out with a true sense of grace and gratitude. That was Kris's story. Little was I aware how her glowing inner spirit would radiate and touch my life. Never before did scripture become so alive and real "...*let your light shine before others, that they may see your good deeds and glorify your Father in heaven.*" (Matthew 5:16, NIV)

To hear Kris's story of being born with numerous congenital malformities, multiple surgeries, and the many hours at doctor offices and in the hospital is, at its simplest level, mind staggering. I think the average person would be left with a sense of being abandoned, unloved, and bitter. Yet, what I saw in Kris was a person who embraced challenges with a spirit of thanksgiving and joy. I did not see someone who was physically different than most. I did not encounter someone who took advantage of her every right to be angry. I didn't experience someone with a chip on her shoulder. What clearly came through in her presence and attitude was a person who loved life, found strength in the midst of misfortune rather than dwelling in self-pity, reached out to others with care and compassion, and praised the Lord with all her heart, mind, and soul. This again brought scripture to life.

Jesus replied: "Love the Lord your God with all your heart and with all your soul and with all your mind." (Matthew 22:37, NIV)

Kris's spirit is infectious! People are drawn to her because they too notice the beaming smile on her face and the joyous bounce in her step. There is something special, something different. People come to love and trust her because she accepts them as Christ embraces us all, with love and grace. I give thanks daily that she has accepted me with all my shortcomings - believe me, they are numerous - and has allowed me to share in her life. By the time Kris and I were married she had endured over 30 surgeries.

More than 20 years have passed since that day we first met. I have witnessed Kris's continual growth in her faith. We have walked together through some twelve - plus surgeries and many more hospitalizations. We have been to Denver for special ethanol ablations to stop the ever-growing vascular network that looks more like a tangled bowl of spaghetti than a creative network of blood-carrying vessels. We have journeyed to the Mayo Clinic in Rochester, Minnesota for a week-long series of comprehensive tests and visits with more specialists than some people see in a lifetime. By this time Kris had suffered four pulmonary embolisms, yet we walked away from the Mayo Clinic with no answers. Finally, we were pointed to a renowned geneticist who would review her case and analyze her DNA. After all these years, there had never been a specific diagnosis for Kris's condition. In 2002 it was finally determined that Kris had a rare disease known as Proteus-like Syndrome, a disease that will eventually take her life.

Since that diagnosis her physical condition has continued to decline. She is on multiple medications to control pain as her muscular and skeletal systems deteriorate. She now has to utilize a motorized scooter to get around for longer distances or periods of time. The reality is that eventually, far sooner than we would hope, she will be confined to it. She also is on Coumadin at a level about two to three times that of the average patient to keep her blood thin enough to minimize the possibility of additional pulmonary embolisms. Pulmonary emboli are the number one cause of death in Proteus patients.

Through all this - through the daily pain, fear, and reality of death's knock at any time - Kris's spirit and faith remain strong! The beaming smile and effervescent personality that greeted me in the parking lot some twenty-two years ago is wider and bubblier than ever. I have been touched by her spirit and am amazed at her courage! I have been comforted by her compassion and companionship. I have been honored to share in ministry together. I am blessed to share in this journey! I have experienced through Kris's life and actions what it truly means to *"let your light shine" (Matthew 5:16, NIV)* and not to let the evil one blow it out! For God proclaims *"I am making everything new!" (Revelation 21:5, NIV)*

The Spirit of Noah

A number of years ago, it began. It really started out slowly as if no one could notice it at all, including me. Then, the speed began to pick up as if rolling quickly down a steep hill. Before I knew it, my office, home, and wardrobe were flooded. It became the desire of family, friends, parishioners, students, acquaintances, and even friends of family members whom I really didn't know. The collection of Noah's Ark! It is a collection that continues to grow and includes some one-of-a-kind arks. For a while, it seemed that everyone was adding to my collection but me. In fact, going through my collection, piece by piece, I learned that indeed, I personally added only one item to my collection over the years.

Fortunately, I love the story of Noah's Ark! In fact, it is my favorite story in the Bible. Many who think they know me believe that because I love children and worked so many years with them that this explains why I love the story - oh, plus the cute little animals. In reality, while it is a great story and the animals are cute, that has nothing to do with my love of Noah. This story made a big impact on my life as a child. Along with other students, I not only learned the story well, I also learned all the extra details and presented what I had learned to our congregation and community. As I did, the Spirit of Noah filled me.

I was in grade school when our church music program was booming. We took months to prepare the stage production of "100% Chance of Rain" by Walter S. Horsley. Each of us learned the songs and script, and we also helped the adults with making costumes and building sets. Some of the songs still ring clearly in my head. On the other hand, the message of the story is cemented on my heart!

Prior to sharing how my heart was changed by this beloved story, it is important to have some working knowledge of what the Bible says about it. By the time of Noah, God had long since created the heavens and the earth, water and land, plants, animals, and mankind to watch over and care for them. Unfortunately, mankind began to ruin the good things God had created. Mankind did not care for that which was placed in their care. In their greed and dishonesty, they disobeyed God. Mankind had turned away from God and became corrupt.

> *The Lord saw how great the wickedness of the human race had become on the earth, and that every inclination of the thoughts of the human heart was only evil all the time. The Lord regretted that he had made human beings on the earth, and his heart was deeply troubled. So the Lord said, "I will wipe from the face of the earth the human race I have created—and with them the animals, the birds and the creatures that move along the ground—for I regret that I have made them." But Noah found favor in the eyes of the Lord. This is the account of Noah and his family. Noah was a righteous man, blameless among the people of his time, and he walked faithfully with God. (Genesis 6:5-9, NIV)*

So, needless to say, the earth was quite a mess and God was very angry. God gave directions to mankind and mankind didn't follow through with them, except for one man—Noah! God then told Noah to build an ark. God provided extremely specific instructions which included the exact measurements required. Noah then followed God's blueprint down to the length and type of wood used to build the ark. God told Noah He was going to send a great flood to destroy all that the earth contained, except for Noah, his family, and the animals on the ark. Early on in the ark building process, God told Noah that there would be a promise in this horrific flood. It is hard to imagine being Noah, the only one on earth who had done what God asked. God was extremely angry with mankind. The earth would never be the same again.

> *Noah did everything just as God commanded him.*
> *(Genesis 6:22, NIV)*

The flood came just as God said it would. This flood was greater than any storm any of us can imagine today. It rained and rained and the flood took out everything on the earth, just as God said it would. Who was kept safe and unharmed? Noah and those on the ark, just as God said they would. When the rains died down, the floodwaters began to recede, and the land began to dry, God brought beauty and His promise. God put a rainbow in the sky to signify the promise God made that day. God agreed that from that day forward, He would NEVER flood the earth again and destroy all living things. It is difficult to hear this story and not wonder how God would have seen me if I lived in Noah's time. I wish I listened better than I do. I pray for strength, compassion, and peace. I desire for God's will to be my will, but I still mess up - OFTEN! Would I too have been in the group destroyed? Probably, as difficult as that is to process.

This is what my heart has sealed upon it: as angry as God was, He still had hope for the future. God still believed that people could follow God's command and listen to directions. God believed this even before the flood. God believed goodness would indeed come. God put a beautiful rainbow, filled with color beyond imagination in the sky between the grey and white clouds that had brought destruction. This was God's promise! As difficult as life becomes, as misdirected, confused, and alone as we may sometimes feel, God will always bring goodness out of the storm. At some point, the storm will be broken and the rainbow will shine brightly in the sky to redirect the heart.

In the past 20 years, I have had the opportunity to speak, teach, and preach on the Scripture reading from Genesis regarding Noah and his ark numerous times. Many times my supervisor would assign me the text, solely because it was my favorite. Throughout the years of preaching I learned not to rely solely on my speaking ability that was refined throughout college and seminary. I quickly learned that the Spirit of God had much more to say than I could ever put together on my own. This meant during my study, prayer, and preparation I would come to know the general direction I anticipated taking. It also meant that I left a lot of room for the Spirit to work, including the possibility of changing everything I thought I would say that day to make room for what God really wanted to be communicated. There have been numerous times I was quoted as saying something in a class or sermon that was not even close what I planned to say. Many times there was no correlation with my notes. I knew each time that God had truly intervened and taken over, because I could never have come up with any of the material myself.

The last time I recall preaching on the Noah story was profound for me. I was in the midst of a very difficult situation with important decisions hanging in the balance. I was a bit uncomfortable preaching on this part of scripture, especially when I still didn't know the outcome of my own situation. Once again, God directed my words and I ended my sermon with the phrase, "Accept God's Challenges, Believe God's Promises!" In the midst of my own struggle, God used my own message to speak to me. This was a sobering experience which reminded me to never quit looking for the promises of God.

Between the notebooks and banners, music boxes and figurines, rugs and garland, ornaments and salt & pepper shakers, shirts, vests, overalls, and sweatshirts, to the largest (let's put a battery in it and float it in the lake) and the tiniest (that looks minuscule in the palm of my small hand) my space is always flooded with reminders of the rainbow. The rainbow and what it signifies is what is etched on my heart. When I believe I am fighting my greatest battles, God will always be there to remind me that I don't have to have all the answers because His promises will endure - forever! Join me in accepting God's challenges and believing God's promises.

Scars of Truth

A brilliant, yet anonymous, person once said, "Scars tell a better story than tattoos." I believe the person who made this profound statement understood with great magnitude the impact scars have on life. Each of us has scars. Some are literal and can be seen with the human eye. They serve as a visible reminder of an injury or surgery. The physical mark of a scar, be it narrow or wide, thick or even with the surface of the skin, is a permanent, physical reminder of a painful experience. Other scars hide within the story of the one wounded. These scars may come from a relationship gone bad, feelings hurt, being taken advantage of, or enduring life's disappointments, difficulties, or milestones.

Any way you look at it, scars are a reminder of pain endured. Regardless of the type of scar, how the pain was inflicted, or how long it took the wound to heal, there was pain at some point in time. Any type of wound takes time to heal as healing is a process. It can be a journey from constant pain to finding less painful yet tolerable moments in the midst of pain. Healing can also represent the hope of finding life again with only reminders of the pain endured. Healing cannot be forced or rushed, but only endured. Day by day. Step by step. Moment by moment. The goal is the same: to heal the wound and find more and more moments that are free from pain.

But regardless, every scar tells a story of a journey traveled. When we take a risk and share our scars - our painful stories - with others, we are likely to have a more complete healing and a better response to the pain endured. When we share the journey of how we obtained our scars with others, we tend to learn more from our journey and have true compassion for others in similar situations. Pain is something that can easily connect people. When we believe someone has traveled a similar, painful journey, they often become instantly credible and are welcomed.

People who have suffered attract those who suffer. Equally, those who have endured attract those who have endured. There is something to be said for those who suffer or have suffered great pain. Pain has the ability to take us to places we never thought we would go. Pain speaks to the innermost parts of our being that we otherwise might never have been connected to.

Healing, in all of its many forms, is needed in our broken world. Sometimes healing the physical parts of our body is easier, because when our feelings and emotions become a part of the equation it becomes more complex and difficult. When a person has a physical scar as a result of an injury or surgery that scar can cause physical pain for years. If a nerve is damaged, there may be healing that never takes place as nerves heal differently than the soft tissue of skin and muscle. To touch a new scar or its surrounding area can send shivers up the spine of the injured person. On the other hand, it can also be a pain-free zone - only time will tell. Complex emotional scars take on a different healing process. Emotional scars can often be a result of layer upon layer of damage. Certainly emotional scars can occur from a single painful experience, but there are times when they are a result of damaging experience after damaging experience.

We live in a world that is always creating and coming up with something different. In the creating we are always searching for something better because we have learned that we deserve the best. The problem is that in our searching for the best, we have also become a very vain people. We want the best and want to be the best in all we do. It is rare for people to pass a mirror and not glance at it to see how they look. In looking in the mirror there is also the opportunity to make a change or improvement to what is reflected in the glass. There is not a morning while getting ready for the day, a drive in the car to run errands, or an evening of watching TV where anyone can escape the cries of the world inviting each of us to become more beautiful. The difficulty is that the beauty the world encourages us to be about is a beauty that is only skin deep. This beauty lasts only a short time and in the process of trying to obtain it, we can undermine efforts to become a better person on the inside. The instant view not only hides the true inner self but also provides an avenue for the true self to permanently remain hidden or even disappear forever.

I did a quick Google search on 'minimizing scars' to find 988,000 results. Seriously, nearly one million places on the internet that can aid me in minimizing my scars? I can't even begin to think about this search engine and the vast places it might take me with further investigation. Where would I begin if I wanted to consider reducing my visible scars? I can reduce them, fade them, or smooth them. The choice is mine. The ads are created to suggest there will be no pain, just flawless beauty on the other side of the treatment.

I have no desire to minimize the appearance of any of my scars. A couple of my early scars have become very small and are nearly impossible to see with the naked eye unless you know where to look. If I were to seriously consider reducing any of my scars, it would mean more money, time, and pain. I am simply unwilling to pay that high a price for the sake of covering up a large part of my life story. Even if money weren't an object, and the procedure was promised to be pain-free and quick, I still can't imagine myself choosing to participate. Why? After all, I have scars from surgical procedures which span my entire body. Some of my scars are more than a ½ inch wide and over 20 inches long. Many are very visible to the naked eye. Most of them are raised above the skin level and leave countless additional scars along both sides from the numerous stitches and staples utilized throughout my lifetime. There are also scars on both hands and forearms from the hundreds of IV's that have been started over the years. The reason I would not venture to reduce my scars is because they are more than a glimpse into my inner self. They are a vital portion of the key to my soul. They also allow an instant connection to others in difficult situations. I am fortunate to have a deep compassion for those in difficult situations because I understand what it means to live through difficulty.

Scars are a deep part of me because they have become an intricate part of my journey-filled life story. Each journey represents the presence of God, a lesson learned, a mountain climbed, and a triumphant glory! If I were to accept any one of the possible treatments to minimize scars, I feel as if I would be turning away from the glory of God. I would end up denying most of my past and find it difficult to find truth in my story. When I tell my story my scars are my truth and reminder of all God has brought me through in this life.

Similarly, when Jesus came to the disciples after His resurrection, His scars spoke volumes. His scars were the evidence they needed to believe He was who He said He was. His scars were the truth they sought. Similarly, Jesus's scars were exactly what Thomas and we often request of Jesus.

Jesus Appears to His Disciples

On the evening of that first day of the week, when the disciples were together, with the doors locked for fear of the Jewish leaders, Jesus came and stood among them and said, "Peace be with you!" After he said this, he showed them his hands and side. The disciples were overjoyed when they saw the Lord.

Again Jesus said, "Peace be with you! As the Father has sent me, I am sending you." And with that he breathed on them and said, "Receive the Holy Spirit. If you forgive anyone's sins, their sins are forgiven; if you do not forgive them, they are not forgiven."

Jesus Appears to Thomas

Now Thomas (also known as Didymus, one of the Twelve, was not with the disciples when Jesus came. So the other disciples told him, "We have seen the Lord!"

But he said to them, "Unless I see the nail marks in his hands and put my finger where the nails were, and put my hand into his side, I will not believe."

A week later his disciples were in the house again, and Thomas was with them. Though the doors were locked, Jesus came and stood among them and said,

"Peace be with you!" Then he said to Thomas, "Put your finger here; see my hands. Reach out your hand and put it into my side. Stop doubting and believe."

Thomas said to him, "My Lord and my God!"

Then Jesus told him, "Because you have seen me, you have believed; blessed are those who have not seen and yet have believed." (John 20:19-29, NIV)

Ultimately in this life, the goal is to find a way to be like Jesus. Scars speak for themselves. Whether there are visible, physical scars or invisible, emotional ones, each represents a story that must be shared. Thomas is a lot like the rest of us. The other disciples had already seen Jesus and the scars He showed them. But Thomas didn't believe their story. In fact he didn't want to simply see the scars on Jesus hands and at His side, he wanted to touch them and put his hand in them.

When we listen to an amazing story, we too want to hear the facts and see the proof. When we see or touch the truth, it becomes more powerful and real. The written facts and the visible proof are the truth we seek. After Jesus's resurrection, He became what His reputation said about Him. Only this time, He had the proof - His scars of truth. It is my hope as well that my scars will be my truth that my journey was accompanied by the hand of God and in the footsteps of Jesus.

Epilogue:
The Journey Continues

Life can change in an instant. For my family it changed when my mom was "presumed guilty until proven innocent" as she was asked what drugs she took while pregnant with me. The question was met with a heartfelt and honest answer. Long before anyone knew I existed, God had entered my life. I have met numerous challenges throughout my life that many will never come close to experiencing. I am not bitter, angry, or resentful. Instead, I am thankful. My heart resounds with words of gratitude because I understand the fullness of God's love and glory. I do not attempt to suggest that I actively see and experience God's glory and love at all times. I know however that God is always near and plays an active role in my life. I have learned something with each challenge and each has made me a stronger person.

I learned a lot from some situations and too little from others. I have found that when I couldn't gain the understanding I needed, the lesson presented itself in another way, down life's winding path. Even in the moments when I thought I wanted to do things on my own, God was still present, nudging me. There was no "losing Him" or "finding Him." Instead, God in His great love and grace has accompanied me throughout my life's journey, and I continue to be overwhelmed by God's continuous, outpouring of gifts.

The Bible comes to life for me and I have related to the words Paul speaks in Romans, where he speaks of suffering in this life and what we should do with it:

> *... we also boast in our sufferings, knowing that suffering produces endurance, and endurance produces character, and character produces hope, and hope does not disappoint us. (Romans 5:3-5a, NRSV)*

The great suffering in my life has produced an endurance that would have otherwise been missing without the hand of God. Each twist and turn that has come in my life, meant that I could develop my character in a positive or negative manner. I believe that because God was invited into my life of suffering, my character chose to remain positive, leading me toward hope. I was taught a long time ago that God's hope would not disappoint me. My suffering, though painful, taught me to endure. This process also developed my character and taught me that hope was always an option. If hope is always a choice, then it cannot disappoint me, ever!

Paul reminds us that none is exempt from life's trials, but each can rejoice in the triumph of God. Paul utilizes words of encouragement punctuated with God's gifts of love and grace to witness to a people who needed to be uplifted. I have taken his words to heart and permitted them to speak to and through my life. I may understand what it means to live a life filled with trials, but more importantly I understand what it means to gain God's triumph and glory despite those trials.

> *I consider that our present sufferings are not worth comparing with the glory that will be revealed in us. (Romans 8:18, NIV)*

It amazes me that God has known all along what I have needed in this life. As God provided His abundant gifts of grace and love, they were gathered to the point of overflowing. God's Word constantly spoke to me. As each lesson was learned I was always brought back to the gift of God's Word. From the beginning, as God's love poured into my life, it never ceased. I lavish in God's continuous gifts and am so thankful.

Because my life was given to God early on, God had many opportunities to triumph over each trial that came my way. God placed me where I needed to be at just the right time, and then placed the right people in my life just when they were needed. Each one aided not only in my survival but also my ability to thrive. Certainly I do not see my life as being even close to perfect, but I see it as very blessed. When God stepped in and carried me through the difficult times. He triumphed. When God led me in the dance and I was ready to make my own debut, He also triumphed. Regardless of my strength, God reigned. Regardless of my faith, God was faithful. Regardless of my hope, God presented reasons for me to be hopeful.

God's blessings are truly unimaginably diverse. Due to God's great love for us our sufferings cannot always be seen with the human eye. The glory of God is of such great magnitude that our hearts and minds of this life cannot comprehend its greatness! That is how vast God's glory is and continues to be. As this life continues to blossom, I intend to appreciate even the trials that come my way. Because of them, God has shown me His triumph. God's triumph can conquer any trial that comes my way. My hope is that you will be continually inspired in your life to seek God's triumph through all the trials that come your way. May God richly bless you, today and always as you continually count your blessings!

CPSIA information can be obtained
at www.ICGtesting.com
Printed in the USA
FSOW02n1131220216
17214FS